He falls well.

He falls well.

A MEMOIR OF SURVIVAL

BY FOLWELL DUNBAR

University of Louisiana at Lafayette Press | 2018

Cover design by Adam Newman
All cover photographs by Scott Saltzman
Flip book art by David Sullivan

ISBN 13 (paper): 978-1-946160-25-6

Library of Congress Cataloging-in-Publication Data

Names: Dunbar, Folwell, author.
Title: He falls well : a memoir of survival / by Folwell Dunbar.
Description: Lafayette, LA : University of Louisiana at Lafayette Press,
    [2018] | Includes bibliographical references and index.
Identifiers: LCCN 2018022447 | ISBN 9781946160256 (alk. paper)
Subjects: LCSH: Dunbar, Folwell. | New Orleans (La.)--Biography. | New
    Orleans (La.)--Social life and customs--21st century--Humor. | LCGFT:
    Autobiographies. | Humor.
Classification: LCC F379.N553 D86 2018 | DDC 976.3/35--dc23
LC record available at https://lccn.loc.gov/2018022447

I stopped to reconnoiter,
only to realize I didn't know what the word meant.

So, I continued on.

Contents

Introduction

Folwell, pronounced "fôl•wel" is, without a doubt, the worst name a wrestler could possibly have. To fall well is to get pinned easily. Whenever my name was announced before a match, there was always a smattering of snickers. Like "A Boy Named Sue" in a singlet, it may have made me tougher—a bit more resilient perhaps? I certainly HATED losing!

As a result, by my senior year in high school I had gone undefeated during the regular season. I set my sights on the Olympics.

But then, I hit a wall. My freshman year in college, I didn't win a match. Not one. And, I got pinned—easily. I was devastated. At the end of the season, I considered quitting. My coach, sensing my frustration and channeling Vince Lombardi (or George Armstrong Custer), said, "It's not how many times you get knocked down; it's how many times you get back up." I had heard the line a number of times, but this time it struck a chord. I got up, learned from my mistakes, trained harder, and, eventually, started winning matches. I never made it to the Olympics, but I did regain lost pride.

Over the years, I've had plenty of "falls" that didn't occur on the wrestling mat. There were pitched battles with older siblings, nasty bouts of dysentery (is there really any other kind?), misadventures overseas, disastrous dates, and numerous near-death experiences.

The worst of these happened just a few years ago (The Fall Guy). I was publicly shamed on the cover of the local paper. The story went viral, and my digital identity was virtually destroyed overnight. Seething in righteous indignation, but unable to respond (or "get back up"), I fell into a deep depression. At times, I was almost catatonic.

My wife suggested that I see a therapist. (She was probably right.) Instead, I came up with my own recovery plan: I would purge myself of "bad experiences," including this one, by writing them all down. "It would be cathartic," I thought. So, at a coffee shop in Antigua, Guatemala, I began jotting down notes.

From the bayous of south Louisiana to the headwaters of the Amazon, the following are all survival tales. For the sake of explanation, I have also included a story about my namesake and one about my conception (SFW by the way). Finally, there's an updated resume—just in case…

For obvious reasons, this book is dedicated to my wife, Lucia. She's put up with a lot! And, if that weren't enough, she came up with the title.

La Concepción Inmaculada

In the summer of 1989, while waiting in line for a new passport at the Customs Office in New Orleans, I noticed a framed picture on the counter. I immediately recognized the subject. It was the famous sculptor, Enrique Alférez. The picture had been taken about forty years earlier, but he still looked the same. When it was my turn for a photo, I asked the officer why they had used his picture as a model. He said, "Mr. Alférez looks more like a man than any man I ever met."

"True," I said. "He's also the reason I'm here."

———

In the late twentieth century, just about every old Mexican claimed to have fought with Pancho Villa. But when PBS set out to make a documentary on the revolutionary hero, they had trouble finding anyone who actually had— until they met Señor Alférez. Enrique spent almost ten years riding with Villa. He used to tell me that to survive in the desert, they had to eat people. He said the knuckles were particularly tasty.

After his stint fighting along the border, Alférez moved to Chicago where he studied art and cleaned skyscraper windows. On his way back to the Yucatan, he stopped in

In Mexico. From left to right: George Dunbar, Jane Dunbar,
Enrique Alférez, Shearly Grode, Peggy Alférez, and Bob Helmer

New Orleans and, like so many others, never left.

Enrique and my father shared a studio in Gallier Hall and became fast friends. According to my dad, "If only half the stories were true, he'd still be the most interesting man I ever met." Alférez married nine times, picked fights with people of "questionable character," spent numerous nights behind bars and, of course, even though he was colorblind, created some of the most endearing works of public art in the city of New Orleans.

Ricky, as he was called by his friends, was always working. Along with my dad, he was the most prolific artist I ever met. He was also very opinionated. Check out his duck, for Huey Long's infamous deduct box at Charity Hospital, or his Latin American David on Poydras Street. He used to tell me, "You know Folwell, your (expletive) countrymen are sons of bitches (long pause with a scowl), but so are mine!"

A devout atheist, Ricky lived in a church on Eighth Street. It was part of a compound that included a couple of houses, a tall cement wall with broken bottles embedded across the top, and a large courtyard with unfinished sculptures and avocado trees. Strangely, he had an almost identical compound down in Morelia, Mexico. At least twice a year he and his last wife, Peggy, would drive down to cast sculptures and to escape the weather and madness of New Orleans. They would also smuggle pharmaceuticals to the local hospitals where there were frequent shortages of antibiotics.

In the winter of 1965, they asked my mom to join them. She imagined walking the beaches of Puerto Vallarta with Tennessee Williams or sipping mescal under the volcano with Malcolm Lowry. She immediately (and foolishly) said, "Yes!"

My mom was a rare and delicate flower. She was petite with pale green eyes and olive-colored skin. For her, "roughing it" was making groceries at Schwegmann's or reading a magazine on the porch. She was definitely not cut out for transporting art and drugs across the Rio Grande.

Ricky and Peggy had an old Bronco and a beat-up trailer. Neither one was all that roadworthy, especially for the roads of Mexico, which were, at the time—it's hard to believe—even worse than the streets of New Orleans. For almost two weeks, with my mother in tow, they bounced over potholes and boulders, Aztec ruins and blue agave, making their way from the Big Easy to Morelia. There were countless breakdowns and flat tires, bribes to *la policía y los bandi-*

dos, and painful bouts with a vengeful Montezuma.

Avoiding General John "Black Jack" Pershing with Pancho Villa would have been an easier feat! The trip was one endless Day of the Dead!

When they finally arrived in Morelia, my mom was a mere shadow of her former shadow-like self. She called my dad in tears. "I made a terrible mistake," she cried. "I should never have come!"

"Sweetheart, everything will be OK," my dad assured her. "I'm wiring money now for a flight to the capital. I'll book us a room at the Gran Hotel Ciudad de Mexico on the Zocalo. I'll see you there tonight."

My parents hadn't planned on having another child. Two was enough. Nonetheless, nine months later, I was born.

It was a *concepción inmaculada*—with a little help from the manly Mexican in the picture frame.

My mom and dad in Mexico City, ca. 1965, the year I was conceived

For a Namesake
The Origins of Falling Well

Emile

I was named after my great uncle, Emile Folwell Legendre. Because he had five sisters, everyone knew him as "Brother."

He died just before I was born.

"I think Brother may have invented tailgating," my father told me. "He never missed a Tulane game. He would set up hours before, and serve food and drinks from the back of his station wagon to anyone who was interested. After the game, win or lose, he'd do it all over again. Everyone loved Brother."

"So, is that why you named me after him?" I asked.

"No," my father said, "it was because he was a good man."

"He would always buy extra tickets and give them to kids outside the stadium. At an Ole Miss game in Oxford, several Rebel fans confronted Brother in the stands."

"We're not gonna sit next to a bunch of black kids," they complained.

"Then you'll have to find somewhere else to sit," Brother said. "They're with me."

"Yes," my father said, "your great uncle was a good man."

Timothy

My parents weren't big fans of organized religion, but they loved Father Tim. He was the parish priest for a small town just outside New Orleans. He was a big man with a big personality. He drank and laughed a lot.

At a cocktail party, he pulled my parents aside and reminded them that I still needed to be baptized. Out of respect and affection for Father Tim, my mom and dad reluctantly agreed.

The following Sunday, my parents dressed me in all white and took me to the church for the first time. My mom walked me up to the altar and presented me to the priest.

"What is your son's name?" Father Tim asked.

"Folwell," my mom said.

"Paul?" he clarified.

"No," my mom said, "it's Folwell with an 'F.'"

Father Tim leaned toward my mother and whispered in her ear, "Jane, I'm sorry, but Folwell is not a Christian name. Does he have a middle name?"

"Yes," my mom said proudly, "it's Legendre."

"Do you mean 'John?'" Father Tim asked.

"No, Legendre, L-E-G-E-N-D-R-E," she said.

"Jane, I'm sorry but that's not a Christian name either," Father Tim said with a sigh.

Without skipping a beat, my mom said, "Well, his Christian name is Timothy, after you of course."

The priest smiled, and then doused my head in holy water.

Celeste

When I was in college, my father called me up and told me I needed to come home. He said Celeste, Brother Legendre's widow, was terminally ill. He wanted me to see her before she died.

Apart from my baptism twenty-two years earlier, I had never met Celeste. The only things I knew about her were that she had earned a Ph.D. and that she lived in Hammond, Louisiana.

When I arrived at the hospital, a nurse told me that Celeste had slipped into a coma. She had been unresponsive for more than two days. Sitting next to her bed, I didn't know what to do or say. It was awkward. Finally, I reached over and held her hand. When I did, she opened her eyes and turned her head. "I have something for you," she said.

She grabbed a framed photograph of my great uncle from the side table and handed it to me. "I've always wanted you to have this," she murmured. She squeezed my hand, smiled, and then closed her eyes.

The next day she died.

Folwell

Folwell wasn't exactly an easy name to grow up with. Kids teased me, and adults would always ask me the same two questions: "Like Jerry?" and "Is that a family name?" (I would always respond: "No, different spelling and ideology." And, "No, my parents found it in a book

Emile "Brother" Folwell Legendre, my namesake

at the checkout counter at Schwegmann's.") I also later
discovered that it wasn't exactly the best name to have as
a wrestler.

Needless to say, over the years I acquired a number
of nicknames, including Foly, Fuzzy, Foz, Fu, and Fubear.

Still, I prefer "Folwell," the one from my namesake.

Cowboys & Indians, Harry Houdini, & the Aspiring Jockey

It was one of the meanest rat snakes I had ever caught. It bit me three times before I was able to grab it behind its diamond-shaped head.

I quickly dispatched it into my sister's room, dropped it into her jewelry box, and closed the lid.

"Vomit face!" I yelled. "Guess what? I found those earrings you lost. I put 'em back in your box."

My sister loved jewelry, but she wasn't terribly fond of snakes.

Even though we lived in Slidell, Louisiana, her scream could be heard all the way in Bay Saint Louis, Mississippi!

My brother was talking to our father in the driveway. Without saying a word, I walked up to them, clinched my fist, and punched my brother as hard as I could square in the nose. There was nothing but blood and tears.

I knew I'd get in trouble; but, I also knew I wouldn't get killed—at least not then and there. When my brother finally stopped crying, he pulled me aside and snarled, "I'm gonna beat you up for an hour every day for a week." I nodded my head and smiled; it was still worth it.

Cowboys & Indians

"Hey Zitmeat, ya wanna play Cowboys and Indians?" my brother and sister asked. "We'll even let YOU
be the cowboy!"

"Really?!" I said.

I was six years old at the time and, like most six-year-
olds, desperately wanted to *be* a cowboy. I had just seen the
movie, *True Grit*, starring John Wayne and Glen Camp-
bell. I envisioned myself galloping across the plains, reins
clinched in my teeth and guns blazing.

I laced up my Buster Brown boots, put on my Roy
Rogers hat, and grabbed my Daisy BB gun. I was pumped
up like a Westminster poodle!

"The Indians here lived on the other side of the bayou," my siblings told me. So, we jumped in a pirogue and
paddled across. There, too far from home to protest, my
brother and sister informed me that I was their prisoner.
According to them, cowboys had been notoriously cruel
to Native Americans. They mentioned a Trail of Tears
and a Wounded Knee. "You and all the other cowboys
deserve to be punished," they said.

So, they tied me to a loblolly pine with bridle leather,
baling twine, and duct tape. Then, they took off all my
clothes, saying it was a Choctaw tradition. "You're lucky
we didn't scalp you," they yelled from the pirogue as they
paddled away.

Facing passing boats in all my prepubescent glory, I
spent the next hour and a half gnawing my way free.

Survivor's note: When I finally escaped, I swam across
the bayou, grabbed a can of Raid Yard Guard insect

repellent, and attacked my Indian assailants. And, like Custer at Little Bighorn, *I* got in trouble!

Harry Houdini

"Tying you up to a tree was a test," my brother later confessed. "And, you passed! We were so impressed; we think YOU could be the next Harry Houdini."

"Who?" I asked.

"Harry Houdini," my brother said. "He was the greatest escape artist of all time. YOU could be an escape artist too."

"Really?!" I said. "What do I need to do?"

"Practice," my brother said. "Practice makes perfect. And, you'll need an incentive."

"What's an incentive?" I asked. (My brother was four years older and obviously had a far more extensive vocabulary.)

"An incentive is why you do things," he said. "Houdini escaped for fame and fortune. And, of course, to avoid death. Until you get rich and famous like him, your incentive will have to be staying alive." (My brother failed to mention how Houdini had died!)

My father had an artesian well-water pool. The water was ice cold and pitch black. My brother tied me to a teak chaise lounge chair and tossed me in the deep end. Squirming at the bottom, I somehow managed to stand upright with the chair on my back. Like Tigger from the house of Winnie the Pooh, I pogoed my way toward the shallow end. About halfway there, I bounced just high enough to break the surface and gulp much needed air. Near the stairs, I finally wriggled my way free.

By the "Houdini" pool, ca. 1969

"Nice job," my brother said, "but that was way too easy. If you're to be the next Harry Houdini, you're gonna need something more challenging." He then tied me to a metal chair, tied the chair to the underside of the diving board, and left me alone with nothing—but a strong incentive.

Over the course of my "training," my brother locked me in a chicken coop with an ornery rooster, put me in a running dryer with only two pillows, buried me up to my chin in creosote contaminated bayou sludge (I sometimes glow at night and bugs want nothing to do with me.), and left me in a hole so deep I had to dig an escape tunnel like El Chapo. And no, I never got rich or famous, though I did manage to stay alive—barely.

The Aspiring Jockey

"Like you, Houdini was small," my sister said. "If he hadn't been an escape artist, he would have made a great jockey. YOU could be a great jockey!"

"Really?!" I said. (The gullibility of youth has no limits.)

"Yes," she said. "But, of course, you'll need to practice…"

My sister was an excellent equestrian, was much older and wiser than me and, I think, had just finished the book,

Zen in the Art of Archery by Eugen Herrigel. "To become a great jockey," she said, "you have to become ONE with the animal. You have to BE the horse. To accomplish this, you'll need to learn to ride without a saddle or a bridle."

We had a Shetland pony named Frisky. Frisky was, well, true to her name. My sister plunked me on her back and advised me to hold on to her shaggy mane for my dear life. She then thumped Frisky on her rump with a switch and the pony took off like a thoroughbred.

I'm pretty sure Frisky knew exactly where she was going: a fresh clover patch on the other side of the property. And, I think she had a plan for how to ditch an unwanted rider.

On my horse Frisky, ca. 1975

Along the way there was an enormous longleaf pine. It had one giant limb that ran perfectly parallel to the ground. It was about a hand taller than Frisky, in other words, level with my solar plexus. Frisky ran straight for it.

Hanging from the limb by my ribcage and desperately gasping for breath, I began to plot my revenge. Later that day I would hunt for snakes and practice my uppercut.

———

Survivor's note: Over the span of my childhood, my older brother and sister shot me with a Benjamin Pump Air Rifle (I had to pick out the pellet from my thigh with a Swiss Army knife!), put poison ivy, cayenne pepper, and fire ants in my underwear, abandoned me on a buoy in the middle of Lake Pontchartrain, and sold my horse while I was away at summer camp. And, as you will discover, they told me I was Hitler's son. Adulthood, with its taxes, Trumps, and colonoscopies, has been a leisurely walk in Audubon Park!

U-Boats on the Bayou

During a college interview, I was asked, "So, Mr. Dunbar, how many siblings do you have?"

I drew a complete blank. There was a long awkward pause before I finally, hesitantly replied, "Just two."

When the interviewer asked why it had taken so long to answer, I responded without delay, "U-boats."

———

I grew up on Bayou Bonfouca just outside of Slidell, Louisiana. My dad had bought an old tomato farm that ran along the meandering waterway. To protect the shore from erosion and errant boats, he had built a bulkhead with large chunks of broken cement and cracked granite. As a child, I would patrol the banks looking for snakes and turtles. The reptiles loved to sun themselves on the hot rocks.

One day while walking along the edge of the bayou with my brother, I discovered a rusty piece of mangled metal sticking out of the shallows. "What's that?" I asked excitedly.

"It's a U-boat," my brother said.

"What's a U-boat?" I asked

"U-boats were German submarines. The Nazis used them to sink Allied ships during the war. They attacked

Riding on my dad's shoulders, ca. 1968

merchant ships too, some here in Louisiana." My brother was four years older and, apparently, knew a lot of history.

"And they came up the bayou?" I asked.

"Not usually," he said, "but this one was special. It was the one that brought you here."

"What do you mean?" I stammered.

"Well," he explained, "the war was going badly for the Germans. They had lost North Africa, Italy and Stalingrad; the Americans and Russians were closing in on Berlin. The Führer was running low on arms and ammunition. To sustain the offensive, he desperately needed cash. So, he sold his only son to the Allies. Dad agreed to adopt you. A U-boat brought you here. It got stuck in the mud, and, well, the rest is history."

Sensing my lingering doubt and impending agony, he said, "Yes, *you* are Hitler's son."

I was seven years old at the time. I only knew a few things about the war: we had been attacked at Pearl Harbor; we fought the Germans and Japanese and won; and Hitler was evil.

Like torpedoes from a submarine, tears shot from my head.

While I cried hysterically, my brother lobbed a historical hand grenade over my head. He said, "Selling you actually funded the Battle of the Bulge. You should be ashamed." He shook his head and walked away.

When I finally stopped crying, I ran to my sister. She was older and more mature. Surely, she would tell me the truth.

My sister calmly listened as I sniffled my way through the story. When I finished, she put a gentle hand on my shoulder, looked into my glassy eyes, and said in a calm, sympathetic voice, "Yes, it's true, Hitler was your father."

Once again, tears welled up and cascaded down my flushed cheeks.

"Why do you think I named my dog Eva?" my sister asked rhetorically over my cries. "Eva Braun was your mother."

The news was devastating, but I still wasn't convinced it was true. My brother and sister (and I) were prone to telling fibs. "No Dad, I didn't put firecrackers in figs and then feed them to the chickens. No, mom, I didn't put a tree snake in the ficus. Of course, we wouldn't call the neighbors and ask them if their toilet was running!"

To learn the truth, I knew I had to go to the source. I had to ask my dad. But, I also knew he would surely deny the allegations. He would never admit that I was Hitler's son. So, instead, I asked him about the U-boats.

Having served in the war and being a bit of a history buff, he happily entertained the question.

"Yes, there were definitely German submarines in the Gulf," he said. "There were numerous reports in *The Times-Picayune*. Ernest Hemmingway, my favorite author, used to look for them off the coast of Cuba in his beloved boat, the *Pilar*. They could have entered Lake Pontchartrain through the Rigolets, but the water in the lake is awfully shallow. If a U-boat had come up the bayou, it would have gotten stuck. You'd probably find its rusty remains in the mud."

My heart sank like a submarine.

I cried for about a week. Then, I had an epiphany: "If my dad was willing to adopt Hitler's son, he must truly love me." He did—and everything was OK.

Hitler's son at home, ca. 1976

Epilogue

It wasn't until years later when my math skills had improved that I realized that Hitler could not have been my father. He died* over twenty years before I was born—at Baptist Hospital on Napoleon Avenue.

When I studied history in high school and college I learned that Hitler and Eva Braun had not had children, and that the Battle of the Bulge had not been underwritten by the sale of a child. And, I later discovered that the rusty metal in the bayou was from a barge that had been

---

*My brother later tried to convince me that Hitler had survived the war and had fled to South America. It was there that he tried to revive the Third Reich by selling me to dad. He mentioned the film, *The Boys from Brazil*. "You," he proclaimed, "are from Brazil!"

used to transport Saint Joe bricks to New Orleans.

I recently visited the National World War II Museum to see the exhibit, "The Road to Berlin." I'm happy to report there was no mention of me.

My brother and sister later retracted the story. They said they were just trying to make me tough; it was part of my "education."

From this experience, I learned the true value of math, the importance of studying history, and the difficult, sometimes disturbing, meaning of the word, "sibling."

The Earworm[*]

Over the course of my life, I've had a number of frightening experiences, from learning that I was Hitler's son, to being diagnosed with five lesions on my left lung, to falling off the world's tallest active volcano. I've also had a number of painful ones. They included having reams of gauze rammed up my fractured nose, surviving numerous bouts of Montezuma's Revenge, and spilling Jalapeño juice on a rather sensitive part of my anatomy. Rarely though, have these experiences been both frightening and painful at the same time—that is, with the exception of the earworm.

———

I grew up on a small farm just outside of New Orleans. We raised horses, goats, and chickens, and we grew tomatoes, bell peppers, and figs. I had a number of chores.

---

[*] There are more than 350,000 species of known beetles, that's one-fourth of all creatures on the planet! The larval stage of a beetle is commonly referred to as a grub or a worm. While there is an order of insects called earwigs and a moth caterpillar called a corn earworm, there is no earworm among the many beetles. I used the term for the title because of the euphemism for a song that gets stuck in your head. Considering what happened to me, both the grub invasion as well as the paranoia brought about by my sibling's deliberate misinformation, I figured the term was nonetheless accurate.

With my dad and sister, ca. 1969

They included collecting the eggs, cleaning out the stalls, guarding the fig orchard against marauding birds, and plucking downy feathers from prepubescent squab.

My least favorite, even more so than removing baby pigeon feathers, was weeding the garden. The job was excruciatingly tedious. I would pull up a clump of weeds, shake off the dirt, and then toss it into a wheelbarrow—again, and again and again. When the wheelbarrow was finally full, I would empty it into the composting bin, or feed the contents to our ravenous and appreciative chickens.

One day while I was working in the garden, I shook a large clump of torpedo grass above my head and a clod of dirt sailed into my ear. I tried to dig it out with my index finger, but instead, I forced the dirt deeper inside. Then, the clod mysteriously began to move. I screamed like Shelley Duvall in *The Shining,* and ran for the house.

My mom did what just about any mother would do: she prodded me with a Q-tip and then poured alcohol down my ear. This, of course, only frightened the alien invader inside. To escape the miniature ramrod and stinging liquid, it bored deeper into my skull. Eventually, it reached those three little bones you learn about in high school biology class, and it started pounding them like Rocky Balboa in a meat locker.

The sparring produced a deafening cacophony, seemingly consisting of 1) fingernails on a blackboard, 2) a wailing baby on a red-eye flight, 3) a jackhammer, 4) a car alarm, and 5) a riverboat calliope that played the same &%$# song over and over again. Only my own glass-shattering shrieks rivaled the tortuous racket inside my head.

My parents threw me in the back of the family station wagon and rushed me off to Slidell Memorial Hospital. There, a doctor used a number of sinister tools and foul-smelling chemicals to extract the creature burrowing into my brain.

"Looks like a juicy grub found its way into your inner ear," exclaimed the doctor. "Poor little fella, he musta been terrified in there." Author's Note: If I had known the meaning of the expression "bedside manner" and the definition of the word "empathy" (and if there had been an internet at the time), I would have given the doctor a piss-poor rating on Healthgrades.com.

Back home, once I had stopped whimpering, my older sister whispered in my good ear a line she had lifted from *The Twilight Zone*: "Yeah, the doctor may have gotten the grub, but it was a female and she definitely laid eggs!" Tears immediately welled up, and I resumed my whimpering.

My parents tried to console me by telling me it wasn't true, but my sister was sadistically persistent. After a week or so had passed, she pulled me aside and said, with an air of authority, "They're probably just dormant." I didn't know what the word, "dormant" meant, but I figured it out using context clues from her follow-up statement: "You know cicadas can stay under ground for years! You could be in high school by the time the little zombies hatch."

So, I lived in abject fear for almost two years. It wasn't until fourth grade that my sister's claims were definitively debunked. My teacher, Mrs. Grey, did a unit on life cycles. She brought in all kinds of critters. There were guinea pigs, turtles, frogs, and butterflies. She also brought in a terrarium with different types of beetles. She explained how the adult beetle laid eggs in the soil or a rotting log. "After a while," she said, "the larvae hatch. They root around in the soil for weeks or even months, eating and growing. Then they pupate and become pupa." We, of course, all snickered when we heard, "pupate." She quickly brought us back to attention and continued, "After a time, the adult beetles emerge. The process is called 'metamorphosis.' Don't be surprised if this term shows up on your next spelling test."

I raised my hand and asked, "Can a beetle larva lay eggs?"

"No, Folwell," she said, "only the adult female can." I ran up to Mrs. Grey and gave her a big hug. I had never been so happy to learn something new!**

———

While swimming in the bayou later that summer, something nicked my upper thigh. "That's not good," my older brother said. "I hate ta tell ya, but it was probably a candiru."

What's a candiru?" I asked.

"I'm not sure you want to know," he replied. But then, of course, he proceeded to tell me—in gory, exaggerated detail…

** In the world of education, we often talk about the importance of rigor and relevance. My fourth-grade life cycle lesson was definitely a testament to the latter.

A New Orleans Character
Stories about my Mother

Missing

My mom lived in a tiny apartment in the Lower Garden District. I worked only a few blocks away and would occasionally drop by for a quick bite. One day, I walked in and found my mom sitting silently at the kitchen table. She was wearing her signature black lipstick, a navy-blue bandanna, and, though it was dark inside, tortoiseshell sunglasses the size of sea turtles. She had a cigarette in one hand and a fountain pen in the other. She was staring intensely at a row of pictures and jotting down notes. The pictures, which had been cut out from milk cartons, were of missing children. There were at least a dozen. When I asked her what she was doing, she said, "I'm studying."

"But why?" I asked.

"You see son, many of these kids are much older now. If I am to find them, I have to imagine what they would look like today."

She had a point.

Wrestling Strategies

There were about thirty of us on the Duke wrestling team. We worked out every afternoon for about two and a

My mom, ca. 1960

My mom, ca. 1975

With my mom
during Mardi Gras
in 1989

half hours. Just before practice one day our coach pulled us all together. I assumed it was for a pep talk before our upcoming match against Wake Forest. He had a large cardboard box. He said, "Gentlemen, apparently, we have received a care package. It's addressed to the entire team. It's from Folwell's mother." I simultaneously blushed and cringed. He ripped open the box and poured the contents onto the mat. There were about a hundred individually wrapped Dracula teeth. The card from my mom read, "I thought these would make you look more intimidating." It was signed with black lipstick, "xoxo Jane."

Cooking Tips

My mom never approved of anyone I ever dated. She was a tough, occasionally brutal, critic.

When she met Lucia, who would eventually become my wife, she immediately launched into her usual interrogation:

"So Lucia, do you cook?"

"Not really," she replied. "I actually prefer to go out to eat."

"Do you type?" my mom asked glancing over at her vintage Smith Corona typewriter.

"Not really," said Lucia. "I have to do a lot of hunting and pecking."

"Well then, do you sew?"

"No," she said, "but my sister does."

"So, Lucia," my mom testily demanded, "WHAT DO YOU DO?"

"Apparently, Jane, I make your son happy."

My mom smiled. She had finally met her match.

About a week later, Lucia received a package from my mom. It contained several boxes of JELL-O, a wooden spoon, and an apron. It also contained her calling card with her name crossed out. On the back, she had written, "In case you get confused, there is a 1-800 number."

Sure enough, there is.

If It Weren't for You

We had a chance to celebrate Mother's Day just before my mom died. My brother, sister, and I took her to Galatoire's, her favorite restaurant. At the end of the meal she ceremoniously clanked her wine glass with a butter knife bringing the entire establishment and a few folks on Bourbon Street to attention. In a melodramatic voice, her favorite kind, she exclaimed, "Children (pause for effect), if it weren't for you (another pause accentuated by a muffled cough), I wouldn't BE a mother."

As always, she was spot on.

My mom was a New Orleans character lifted from the pages of a Tennessee Williams play. She could have easily held her own with the likes of Blanche, Maggie, or Stella. While she was alive, I was embarrassed by her eccentricities. Today, I couldn't be prouder. She was a New Orleans original.

Burning Down the House

It was the night before our annual summer trip to Destin, Florida. Todd and I looked forward to it more than Christmas or even Mardi Gras. We were fired up like punks on the Fourth of July.

Todd and I had been best friends since second grade. Although he wasn't my brother, my father treated him like a son. He had been going with us to Florida for the past eight years.

For the first few years, Todd and I spent our time on the beach chasing fiddler crabs and collecting sand dollars. Then, our attention shifted to girls. We would comb the beach like archeologists searching for rare fossils. We had never had any success* (nor would we in the future); nonetheless, we were undeterred.

Partly because of our excitement for the trip, and partly because we had two large Rhodesian ridgebacks in the bed with us, we didn't get to sleep until well after midnight.

---

*Too many years later to actually make a difference, a friend of ours shared the secret to his success. "You bring a football or a Frisbee with you," he said. "When you see a girl you're interested in, you toss it to her. If she catches it and throws it back, you're in like Flynn. If not, you simply continue down the beach."

"That's &%$# brilliant," I said. I then paraphrased George Bernard Shaw and lamented, "Wisdom is definitely wasted on the old."

The house before the fire

My older brother wasn't nearly as excited about the trip. He had just graduated from high school and wanted to stick around with his buddies before they all went off to college. He had gone out to the Time Out Lounge in Old Town Slidell to play pool and drink Dixie longnecks.

He returned home around two in the morning. He was tired and tipsy, but he was also ravenous and loved to cook. (Later in life, he would become an accomplished chef and a successful restaurant owner.) Instead of making something simple like cereal or instant grits, he decided to make a batch of homemade French fries. He poured Crisco Oil into a deep, cast iron skillet, cut up a few Russet potatoes, cranked up the heat, and tossed in the tubers. Then, he got bored with the project. (And, he remembered that he had to drive to Florida in just a few hours.) So, he left the kitchen (and the fries) and retired to his bedroom.

I woke up in the middle of the night. There was a strange scent wafting through the air. I figured one of the dogs was either breathing in my face or had passed gas. But, strangely, the dogs were not there. I got up, walked through the playroom past the entrance to the blazing kitchen, and went back to sleep on a sofa in the living room.

With their acute sense of smell, the dogs had already retreated to the other side of the house. I saw them huddled against the back door like cold squirrels in a warm nest. Unlike Lassie, they had no intention of alerting authorities that the house was on fire (or that Timmy had fallen into the well). They were just looking for a comfortable, smoke-free place to doze.

My sister had been disturbed as well, not by the fire, but by the growling of her stomach. She was suffering from an acute case of the midnight munchies. In a sugar-induced delirium, she walked past the fire, went into the pantry, grabbed a handful of cookies, crawled back to her room on her hands and knees, and climbed back into bed wearing pajamas now covered in crumbs and reeking of charred French fries.

My father, whose bedroom was on the far side of the house, was the last to smell the smoke. He jumped out of bed and charged into the inferno like a fearless first responder. He sounded the alarm, and extinguished the blaze with blankets from his own bed.

We all gathered outside in the parking lot, where we discovered my brother sleeping on the hood of my dad's car. He was wearing only boxer shorts, and he was covered in mosquitoes and sweat.

"What the hell happened?!" my father demanded.

"Not sure," my brother slurred, "I think there may have been a fire?"

"So, you left us all inside to burn?!" my sister barked.

"No," he said, "I went to get help. I must have passed out from all the smoke."

With "all the smoke" still billowing out of the open doors and windows, I suddenly realized that one of our party was missing. "What about Todd?" I yelled!

Todd was a notoriously heavy sleeper. He could crash in the front row of a Who concert. We called him "The Hibernating Sugar Bear." (Note: He also looked like the mascot for Post Golden Crisp Cereal.)

My dad ran back into the smoldering house and found my friend curled up in bed with a mountain of pillows stacked on his head. There was a faint snore punctuated by muffled coughs. Todd's face was the color of soot, but he was still deep in REM—dreaming of girls on the beach no doubt.

Epilogue

For a long time, we gave my brother grief about the fire. "Instead of going to Florida this year," we suggested, "let's just go camping—ON THE HOOD OF A CAR!" Or, "I don't know about you, but we're hungry. Let's make French fries—AND LEAVE!" And, of course, we screamed the refrain from that famous song by the Talking Heads.

It wasn't until many years later that my brother finally fessed up to "Burning Down the House." Enough time had passed, and the smoke of guilt had finally cleared.

A Heart-wrenching Encounter with an Aztec King

When I left Louisiana to attend a boarding school in Massachusetts, my wardrobe consisted of a crusty old Speedo bathing suit and a few stained and tattered t-shirts. My mom affectionately referred to me as "her ragamuffin." Unlike my frog-gigging prowess, my academic skills at the time were limited at best. And, I had never seen snow. At Brooks School in North Andover, students wore a coat and tie to class every day, there were courses like ornithology that I couldn't even pronounce, and it snowed A LOT. I was a choupique out of water. Like the protagonist in Jack London's *To Build a Fire** (a short story I would read later that year), I was definitely NOT going to survive.

And then I met Mandy.

Amanda Coues, as she was formerly known, was a sophomore. She had short, sandy blonde hair, radiant clamshell eyes, and dimples on her cheeks and chin. She looked like the child of Meg Ryan and Dennis Quaid. She had a tomboy gait and an utterly charming smile. From the kitchen crew to the faculty pets, everyone who met her became instantly enamored.

---

* In London's first version, the protagonist survives. As with this tale, a tragic ending was far more compelling.

My crush playing tennis at Brooks School, ca. 1983

And I was no exception. When I saw her, my heart skipped a beat. A budding Bob Dylan devotee, I couldn't stop reciting the lyrics, "If not for you, my sky would fall, rain would gather too / Without your love I'd be nowhere at all / Oh what would I do if not for you?" Yes, I was definitely smitten.

Now that I had a reason to live at this arctic prep school, I had to come up with a strategy for love. There would be flowers of course, chocolates, poems, and puppies. I would make her mixed tapes (with New Orleans R&B and songs from the Hibbing Bard), and I would serenade her outside her dorm room window—in the snow.

Like the Allies before the invasion of Normandy though, I would need months to formulate my master plan. But alas, time was NOT on my side. Nor was Fortuna.

Once a week, the school staged a formal dinner with assigned seating. It was their way to ensure that kids socialized with kids outside their own clique. The day before the first of these tortuous events (and with the assistance of a calculator) I figured out the chances of sitting next to Mandy. They were approximately 133.33 to 1. I liked my odds.

And then, on the next day, the goddess of (mis)fortune dealt me the Queen of Hearts!

Like a mirage, Mandy appeared and sat down directly across from me. She was wearing a beautiful white dress and she had a daisy in her hair. I was wearing an ugly plaid jacket with a mismatched polyester tie. And, to make matters worse, I had a pimple on the end of my nose that I could see without a mirror. Like a slug in the middle of the Bonneville Salt Flats, I was absolutely, utterly terrified.

The menu that night consisted of spaghetti and meatballs (more fear), Caesar salad, and dinner rolls. For a brief moment, I dreamily thought of the restaurant scene from Disney's *Lady and the Tramp* but then determined that the possibility of a noodle-induced kiss was highly unlikely. Worried about drippage and slippage, I would eat pasta without sauce, salad without dressing, and bread without butter.

For beverages, there were three choices: water, milk, and grape juice. I ruled out the first for lack of originality. I liked the second, but it gave me cause for concern. The newly acquired peach fuzz on my upper lip was like catnip to dairy products. The risk of getting a milk mustache was far too great. So, I settled on the third. Though long

before the farm-to-table craze, I liked the idea of support-
ing local Concord grape growers. The drink was also the
color of my favorite flower, the Louisiana iris. I thought
it would look striking against the backdrop of Mandy's
blouse. (*Author's note: This is an obvious and feeble attempt at
foreshadowing, a term I would soon learn from Mr. Spader,*** *my
ninth-grade English teacher.*)

Next, I had to fill my glass. In this, I was as confident
as a show dog. What I lacked academically, I easily made
up for with athleticism. Though small, my eye-hand coordination and strength were both well above average. Like
a seasoned sommelier, I lifted the pitcher and poured the
juice with the utmost precision, even twisting my wrist
at the end to prevent a dribble. Pleased with my performance, I cast my head from side to side fishing for adula-
tion, but there was none. Most of the attention from the
table was directed at the girl in white. Undeterred and
eager to kick-start my nascent courtship, I decided to risk
everything on my favorite joke. "So," I asked, "why did
the chicken cross the road?" After agonizing seconds in a
hailstorm of apathy, I leapt to the punch line: "To prove
to the armadillo*** that it could be done!" There was noth-

**Mandy ended up marrying a friend and classmate of mine. Not
surprisingly, he's a great guy. A quarter of a century later though, I'm
still a bit jealous!

*** In retrospect, I should have gone with "opossum." Unlike the
armadillo, Didelphis virginiana can be found in New England. The
joke would have had a much better chance of succeeding, conceivably
changing the course of history. One of my favorite fun-facts has to do
with armadillos. When the animal is threatened—considering it has no
teeth, this happens a lot—it often leaps straight up in the air. As a result,
when you see one as road kill, it has usually been hit and not run over.

ing but crickets—and renewed attention to the angel with
the flower in her hair.

Sufficiently deterred, I resolved to retreat. I would play
it safe for the rest of the evening. I would simply eat, drink,
and avoid embarrassment at all costs.

Apparently, "all" was not enough. When I reached for the
glass of Concord grape juice, something went terribly awry.
Like an aye-aye's odd middle digit independently probing
for grubs, my pinky finger refused to comply with its more
skilled cohorts. It stuck out like a sore version of its opposable
counterpoint and crashed into the side of the glass. The tall
glass tipped and swiveled on its axes. For a second, I thought
it might catch itself on a crease in the tablecloth. Like a bald
cypress tree with splayed knees, it would swing back erect after the fleeting storm. But it didn't. Instead, it collapsed, ever
so slowly, like the giant in *Jack and the Beanstalk*.

When it finally hit the table, the liquid inside the glass
defied laws of physics.**** Every ounce, every last purple
drop shot from the cylinder—missing the table, chairs,
and floor—and landed squarely on Mandy's white dress.

There was a massive gasp that sucked so much oxygen
out of the room that several people almost fainted. It was
followed by a deafening silence. (A small caterpillar down
by the lake could be heard spinning silk.) All horrified eyes
were on Mandy. She looked like a blue-blooded version
of Sissy Spacek in the movie *Carrie*. Then the eyes, like
daggers, turned to me, the newbie ragamuffin from down
on the bayou.

**** In college, I took a physics course in which I discovered that the
liquid in the glass had indeed defied laws of nature. The phenomena
would have surely caused Sir Isaac Newton to cough up an apple.

It would take years before I would discover the right analogy to describe how I felt at that exact moment. While on a sojourn through Mexico the summer after my sophomore year in college, I came up with this:

Kneeling at the top of Templo Mayor in the Aztec capital of Tenochtitlan, I looked down upon what appeared to be adoring throngs. Quetzalcoatl and Tlaloc were obviously impressed by my bravery, the way I sat directly across the altar from Xochiquetzal, the goddess of beauty and fertility. Then, when the sacrificial cup fortuitously fell to the floor, the great Montezuma drew a macuahuitl or obsidian ax from his jaguar skin scabbard and plunged it deep into my bare chest. He ripped out my still beating heart and cast it down the stairs to raucous cheers. I watched in horror as it tumbled down the stone steps. When it finally reached the ground, it surrendered one final beat, and I collapsed in a mounting pool of blood and tears.

Yep, that's pretty much how I felt.

After the incident, I listened to *Blood On the Tracks*, Bob Dylan's breakup opus until the tape, like my heart, snapped. I was completely "Tangled Up in Blue."

From that day forward, I refused to drink grape juice. And, many years later, while teaching a gaggle of seventh graders about the early engagements of the American Revolution, I only mentioned Lexington.

For the next three years, I avoided Mandy like a Portuguese man o' war, admiring her only from a spill-safe distance. I watched her play tennis from behind the green windscreen on the chain-link fence surrounding the courts; I followed her to class from behind snowdrifts, hedgerows, and trees; and I went to chapel early to sit in the back pew so that I could catch a glimpse of my crush entering the nave. I was like the stalker in that popular song by The Police.

At the end of my junior year, I attended a farewell party for the senior class. As the festivities wound down, I found myself alone on a sofa staring blankly at a stack of coffee table books. "Folwell?" a soft voice enquired. I lifted my head and my heart skipped a beat. It was Mandy, and she was sitting directly across from me again. I quickly surveyed the table to make sure that there were no beverages lying precariously about. I then tried to speak but as always in her presence, my tongue became twisted and tied.

"I'm just curious," she said, "why did you never ask me out?"

Once again, Montezuma raised his obsidian ax.

9 (disastrous) Dates

1. Truth or Dare

It would have been my first kiss.

Maimie was a tomboy, but she was cute as a koala. I was in seventh grade, and she was in sixth. I had a crush on her, and (I think) she liked me.

We were with a group of friends playing Truth or Dare, when one of them "dared" me to kiss her. I lit up like a sparkler, and Maimie blushed like, well, a sixth-grade schoolgirl. We stepped into a dimly lit closet as the others snickered.

Having no precedent, I wasn't sure if I should open my eyes or not. So, I compromised. I squinted like Clint Eastwood in a Spaghetti Western desert. Through the narrow slits, I saw Maimie's puckered face leaning toward mine. It was no longer as cute as an Australian marsupial's though. It looked funny and kinda scary, like a star-nosed mole or a prehistoric pumpkin. It was squinched up as though she had just eaten a half a dozen lemons. I couldn't help it—I'm not proud; I burst out laughing. Maimie opened her eyes, shrieked with embarrassment, and ran away— carrying off any hope of a first kiss!

With my first kiss, Mamie (and her little sister Parish)

2. Eight O'Clocks

At the first Eight O'Clocks dance, I met Comma. (Yes, her name was "Comma." I was ribbed for a solid year with quips like, "Conjunction junction, what's her function," "Semicolon is much prettier," and "I've heard she's a real exclamation point!") I was standing like a wallflower next to the jukebox when she approached. "Do you like music?" she asked.

"Of course," I replied.

"What's your favorite band?" she asked.

"Um, a, um," was all I could come up with. I was more into sports and critters at the time.

"Do you like the Beatles?" she asked.

"I LOVE the Beatles!" I exclaimed.

"So, what's your favorite album?" she asked.

"Um, a, um," I stammered. "I like them all."

"Me too," she said, "but *Rubber Soul* is the best. I LOVE "'Michelle!'"

Before I could respond with something other than "um," a boy stepped in between us and asked her to dance. "Suffragette City" by David Bowie was playing. (I'm haunted by the song to this day!) Comma remained beneath the disco ball with him for the rest of the evening.

At the second Eight O'Clocks, I brought Comma a Dolby cassette of *Rubber Soul*, and I asked the DJ to play "Michelle," not realizing it wasn't exactly an eighth-grade dance favorite.

I then waited, and waited, and waited for *our* song to play, but it never did. Finally, I decided to ask her to dance to something else. I think Queen's "Crazy Little Thing Called Love" was playing. As I slowly shuffled across the floor, absolutely terrified, the song ended, and the DJ announced, "That's it boys and girls. See ya next time!" The lights came on and parents streamed in.

At the third and final Eight O'Clocks, I finally mustered up enough courage to ask Comma out on a date. An actual date! She looked at me with sad blue eyes, shrugged and said, "I wish you had asked me earlier; we're moving back to Stockholm in a week."

Riding home in the back of my parents' faux wood paneled-station wagon, I listened to "Michelle, my bell, these are words that go together well, my Michelle…"

3. The Walk for Hunger

I attended a small New England boarding school. The day before Thanksgiving break, I left a bouquet of flowers in the mailbox of Edie Findeis, a girl I had a crush on. Unbeknownst to me, she had left the day before. When she returned a week and a half later, the flowers (and my first attempt at courtship) had expired!

It took several months to recover. In the spring, I finally tried again. I invited Edie to join me on The Walk for Hunger, an annual charity event in Boston. I had twenty miles to redeem myself for the flower fiasco. Considering Edie was taller, smarter, and way better looking than me, it was gonna be a long, difficult, uphill journey.

Walking along the Charles River, I tried to win her over with my nascent southern charm. I told her Cajun jokes and stories about growing up on the bayou; but both fell painfully flat. Something got lost in translation. I was flailing like a mullet in the dry hull of a Lafitte skiff piloted by Boudreaux and Thibodeaux. So, with my hands buried in my pockets, and looking for any excuse not to look at her, I walked in silence.

Then, I had a revelation. "Maybe I could impress her with my athleticism?" I thought. "I'm on the varsity football and wrestling teams for crying out loud!" But, there was an obvious problem: It was a "walk" and not a "decathlon" for hunger. I would have to improvise.

So, I decided to dazzle her with my stellar skipping prowess. But, as I bounded past Edie, my right foot clipped my left, and, with my hands still stuck in my pockets, I fell like a timber. I landed squarely, face-down in a deep puddle, the only one on the entire path. Embarrassed beyond belief, I wanted to die, possibly from mud water asphyxiation. I lay there motionless, waiting for Edie to laugh, but hoping she would just continue to walk away, far away. But, she didn't, and she didn't. Instead, she helped me up, brushed me off and held my hand. We had more than ten (agonizing) miles to go.

4. The Tennis Match

I met Lisa at a costume party. She was dressed like a punk rocker. When I saw her, I was immediately smitten. We struck up a conversation that eventually turned to tennis. I asked her if she wanted to play the following day. She said, "Yes."

Unfortunately, when we got on the court, my competitive nature trumped my southern sense of chivalry. I dropped, sliced, lobbed, smashed, and taunted my way to a lopsided victory. I won the match, but most certainly lost the date.

The next day in the sports section of our college newspaper, the headlines read: "Dunbar Destroys Hill 6-0, 6-0. Hill Demands Rematch!" Somehow, the relationship still had a pulse.

With my undeserved reprieve, I came up with a new game plan: I invited Lisa to play *with me* in a tournament. She agreed.

At the time, I had a $200 1972 Volkswagen Super Beetle, which, was not exactly "super." The floor beneath the passenger seat had rusted through. I removed the seat and covered the gaping hole with several two-by-fours. I had

My VW Super Beetle, ca. 1988

always wanted a convertible, so I gave a friend of mine, who was a welder, a case of beer to cut off the roof with a blowtorch. When he did, the doors collapsed, so you had to climb over to get in. And, for no particular reason, I painted it to look like a ladybug.

When Lisa saw the car, I'm pretty sure she questioned my boyfriend eligibility. But, being a trooper, she climbed (literally) in and sat in the back.

Lisa looked like she was ready for Wimbledon. She was wearing an adorable white tennis skirt, white Tretorns with white socks, and a white visor. I, however, looked like a ragamuffin. Nothing I was wearing matched, and I had holes in my shoes. If we were ever to become a couple, I would be the Oscar to her Felix.

About halfway there, we hit a huge pothole and muddy water shot up through the repaired floorboard. From visor to Tretorns, Lisa was splattered with mud. She screamed and I down shifted. When I did, the stick shift detached from the car and Lisa screamed again. I popped the clutch, pulled up on the emergency brake, and steered us into a ditch.

Once again, Lisa seriously questioned my eligibility.

5. Moli

Moli was a great dog. She was a cross between a Rottweiler and a pit bull mix. I took her with me to college my senior year. We were inseparable. She went to class, wrestling practice, work, and parties. She was a star wherever she went.

I was taking a philosophy class at the time. (What did the philosophy major say to the engineering student? "How would you like your latte?") The course was structured around a series of Big questions. My debating partner was a feisty pre-law major from the Midwest. She was like the angry spawn of Mary Matalin and James Carville. She could defend any side of any argument—and win.

I enjoyed our sparring so much, I asked her out on a date; which, if you think about it, is the perfect setup for a *Seinfeld* episode.

At dinner, she gave me grief for ordering meat, espousing the many virtues of vegetarianism. At a party, she made us leave because the cover band was playing The Cars. Apparently, their music was sexist. I told her to take it up with Paulina Porizkova. During the walk to

My dog Moli (short for Mona Lisa), ca. 1989

my off-campus apartment, she berated me for belonging to a fraternity. "I'm sure Bluto from *Animal House* is your hero," she said.

"Yep," I agreed. "Seven years of college down the drain. Might as well join the f***ing Peace Corps!"

At my place, we found Moli splayed out in the middle of the bed.

"I'm not sleeping next to a dog," she said.

"But it's her bed too," I pointed out.

"Listen," she said, "all you do is talk about that damn dog. If we're gonna have a relationship, you'll have to choose between me and Moli!"

"Are you kidding?" I said. "I've known Moli since she

was a puppy. I've only known you since the beginning of the semester. She's my best friend. You're my debate partner. There's no argument here! I'll call a cab…"

In the middle of the night, I woke up with Moli's face pressed up against mine. She had really bad breath!

6. Las Cajas

I was a Peace Corps volunteer in Ecuador (see Bluto quote). A colleague of mine, Brian, set me up on a blind date with a woman from Cuenca. Her name was Nidia Vasquez Pesantez. We were going on a hike in Las Cajas, a national park above town.

When I saw Nidia, I immediately realized that she was way out of my league. When she saw me, she immediately realized that I was not dressed for the occasion. The park was over 13,000 feet above sea level, and it was freezing cold. I was wearing shorts, a sweatshirt, and a Saints baseball cap.

About halfway into the hike, it started to rain. A few minutes later, the rain turned to sleet. Soon, I lost feeling in my fingers and toes. And then, above the tree line and far from the nearest public restroom, I suddenly had to pee. But, my fingers were too numb; I couldn't unzip my own pants. It was the perfect storm!

I figured I had two options. One was to simply go in my pants, which, no doubt, would have put a damper on the date, pun intended. The second was to ask for assistance, not from Nidia of course, but from my friend Brian. While potentially far more humiliating, it might just salvage the date. So, I opted for the latter.

When I asked Brian to help, he reluctantly agreed. He unzipped my pants, but I still couldn't manage the equipment. My hands were frozen cod. I had to ask Brian to manipulate my junk!

With a horrified expression on his face, he wincingly obliged. And yes, it DID put a damper on the date!

Author's note: If there were ever a test of friendship, this was it!

Author's Second Note: Brian made me promise never to tell this story—unless of course, it was shared in a memoir many years later, after the statute of limitations had hopefully expired.

7. Salsa Lessons

A friend of mine set me up with an exchange student from El Salvador. We met at Café Istanbul in the Faubourg Marigny. Los Bebes del Merengue were performing a late-night set.

She asked me if I liked to dance. "Of course," I lied. "I LOVE to dance!" In retrospect, I wish she had asked me if I knew HOW to dance. The answer would have been a definitive "No!"

When we stepped out onto the floor, she began to gyrate like Shakira on speed. Her hips defied laws of human physiology. I did everything I could just to stay in front of her.

After a minute or two, the crowd parted like the Red Sea. People surrounded us and started clapping to the music. It was like that famous scene from *Saturday Night Fever*. "Damn, maybe I can dance?" I thought. Then, I realized that all eyes, including mine, were glued to her. She was unbelievable. (I later discovered that she was actually the captain of the National Dance Team of El Salvador.)

By the time the song ended, a line of suitors had formed. It stretched from Frenchmen Street all the way to La Boca in Buenos Aires. Humbled and humiliated, I wilted away into a dark corner like a discarded corsage. I forfeited the floor—and my date.

8. The Colombian Drug Tsar Princess

I told a friend of mine that I wanted to marry a Colombian drug tsar princess. "Being a poor teacher from New Orleans," I somewhat joked, "I'd be the perfect alibi. She could launder her father's dirty pesos at my studio apartment. You know, they say the most beautiful women in the world are from Cali!"

"Really?" my friend said. "A student of mine in the ESL program at Tulane is from Cali. Would you like to meet her?"

"Is Colombian coffee the richest, most aromatic kind?" I said with an espresso shot of sarcasm.

We got together at Le Bon Temps Roule on Magazine Street. True to form, she was obscenely attractive. She was Remedios the Beauty from *100 Years of Solitude*; she was a young Sofía Vergara, only with a less abrasive accent. She was, in other words, my dream date!

Wanting to make an impression, I broke out my rusty Spanish and launched into a monologue about Pablo Escobar, the infamous "King of Cocaine" from Medellín. I figured the topic would be both germane and *divertido* or amusing. It was—and, it wasn't!

"Don Pablo is my hero," I declared! "He steals from the rich and gives to the poor. He's a regular Latin American Robin Hood."

My friend kicked me under the table, but I couldn't stop. I was on a roll.

"I'd love to visit Hacienda Nápoles," I continued. "He's got giraffes, elephants, and hippopotamuses! You know I was once mistaken for Escobar in the jungles of Ecuador! He deserves his own telenovela."

When I finally paused to gauge her response, I saw nothing but icicles in her big brown eyes. She said in coarse, blunt English, "Stop it! ¡*Cállate*! My father is a federal judge in Bogota. Pablo Escobar tried to kill him. He is the devil. Never, NEVER mention his name in my presence again!"

I spent the remainder of the evening trying to dislodge my shoe from my esophagus. Needless to say, I would never *be* in her presence again.

9. The Haircut

I was getting a haircut at Right Up Your Alley on Magazine Street in New Orleans. I had a friend named Gaylynn who worked there. The salon was attached to a coffee shop called Café Luna. Looking out the window, I saw a woman sit down at a table with a tall cappuccino and a newspaper.

"Oh my God," I exclaimed, "I'm in love!"

"You should go talk to her," Gaylynn suggested.

"No," I said, "I've got a better idea. I need to call my friend Zack. He lives just down the street. I'll have him bring her flowers."

Sure enough, Zack appeared within minutes carrying a beautiful bouquet of Louisiana irises. He placed it on the table next to the woman and said, "They're from an admirer." The woman smiled and blushed. She then finished her coffee, got up and left.

"Now what?" said Gaylynne.

"What do you mean?" I asked. "Did you see the smile on her face? It was absolutely radiant!"

"Yea, I know" she said, "but did you get her name and number? Did you ask her out on a DATE?!"

"Oh, oh yeah," I stammered. I felt like Sir Bedivere the Wise from *Monty Python and the Holy Grail*. I had just sent in the Trojan Rabbit, only to realize that I hadn't filled it with brave, chivalrous knights.

I went to Café Luna every day for the next three weeks, but the beautiful woman with the tall cappuccino and newspaper never reappeared.

And then I met my wife. But that's another story…

A Bad Picasso In a Blood-Soaked Singlet

It was my first match at the Bloomsburg Invitational Wrestling Tournament in Bloomsburg, Pennsylvania. Right off the whistle, I shot in for a double leg takedown. Unfortunately, my opponent had the exact same idea and shot only a fraction of a second later. My face and his knee collided head-on. There was a loud "Crunch!" followed by a torrent of blood. My nose was a busted fire hydrant.

The referee stopped the match and my coach ran out onto the mat. "Holy &%$!" he said, "You look like a bad Picasso." He stuffed cotton up my now deformed nose and said, "Try not to wrestle with your face."

I tried, but it didn't work.

In the second period, my opponent hit me with a vicious cross-face cradle, and blood, once again, spewed in all directions. My coach called for the trainer (and a mop). The trainer said, "Holy &%$!, you look like a bad Picasso! Your nose is all over your face!" He plugged the leak with more gauze and told me something I had already figured out on my own: I would have to breathe through my mouth.

By the third period, my blue and white singlet was now the color of a bruised plum, and my nose was so big I

Wrestling at Duke University, ca. 1988

could hardly see. I thought of the scene from *Rocky* where Sylvester Stallone asks Mick to cut him. Then, I remembered, I couldn't afford to lose any more blood.

But I did. A lot. Yet somehow, I managed to win.

For the next two matches, the pattern of bleeding and plugging continued. At one point, I thought I overheard the trainer asking people for their blood type. "Being O Positive was cold comfort," I thought.

Before the semifinals, the referee warned my coach that he would have to call the match if I continued to bleed. Knowing "there will be blood," my coach stuffed even more cotton up my nose and told me to go for a quick pin.

I did. And, in less than twelve seconds, the match was over. The feat, inspired by a face that looked like a cubist painting, would be my only claim to fame as a collegiate wrestler. For almost twenty years I held the record for the fastest pin in Duke University history.

In the finals, I faced (and probably frightened) the number one seed. He was from Penn State, was undefeated, and was, by all accounts, a legitimate Olympic contender. Considering my condition (and the fact that I was very much *unseeded*), my prospects were about as good as my chances of finding a date later that evening. My coach gave me a pep talk, saying I had nothing to lose—except, of course, more blood. "He puts his singlet on just like you," he said, "one leg at a time." (I had my doubts.) "Go for another big move—you'll be like David taking down Goliath!"

"But David could breathe," I thought. "And, he had a sling!"

Off the whistle, I flew into Goliath like a Kamikaze pilot. I latched on to his elbow and armpit and flung myself backwards. The giant sailed over my head and crashed with a "Thud!" His shoulder splintered like a middle school clique, and tears shot from his eyes as he writhed in pain. For the entire first period, I held him on his back, grinding my chin into his shattered collarbone. But, as hard as I tried, I couldn't force his other shoulder against the mat. He was determined not to get pinned.

After the bell, his coach and trainer strongly recommended that he forfeit the match. They told him he needed immediate medical attention, maybe even surgery. When he refused, I knew I was in trouble.

For the next two periods, wrestling with one arm literally tied behind his back, he took me down and let me up, took me down and let me up, again and again. Each time,

he got two points and I got one. When the final whistle
blew, he had won 15 to 14. The referee looked at us both
with a mixture of admiration and pity, and then raised my
opponent's one good arm.

That night, desperate for a diversion and hard up for
cash, I bet my teammates that I would go to the bar in my
underwear if they picked up the tab.

Wearing nothing but boxers and boots, I walked into the
Holiday Inn lounge and sat on a stool at the bar. For whatever reason, perhaps sympathy or shock, the bartender didn't
kick me out. Instead, he asked, "What the hell happened to
you? You look like a bad Picasso. Was it a car wreck?"

"No," I said, "wrestling. You should see the other guy."

"I'd rather not," he said. "What would you like?"

"Something to dull the pain," I said.

"How about a Long Island Iced Tea?" he suggested.

"Make it two," I said.

"Ya got an ID?" he asked.

"What do you think?" I said.

Several hours later, I woke up on the floor next to my
bed gasping for breath. I was drowning in my own blood.
Apparently, my nose, now the size of a Siamese twin,
had decided to send its unwanted liquid to other, more
capable spigots. Like a communist Chia Pet, my mouth,
eyes, ears, and pores were all sprouting red. My roommate
screamed, threw up, and then called for an ambulance.

At the hospital, the ENT looked at me, cringed, and
said, "You look like a bad Picasso. That's one of the worst
breaks I've ever seen. I'm afraid we're gonna have to consult a plastic surgeon."

Waiting on the examination table, I thought about the celebrity noses I most admired. "Maybe I could get a Lee Van Cleef or an Augustus Caesar?" I thought.

When the plastic surgeon arrived, he said, "Holy %$@!, you look like…"

"A bad Picasso," I interrupted. "I know."

"I was actually going to say something else," he said, "but, come to think of it…"

Then, his eyes widened and he exclaimed, "Wait a second—something doesn't seem right." He pulled out a pair of needle nosed pliers the length of a narwhal tusk and plunged it deep into my nasal cavity. Tears flew from my face as I squirmed in horror. I felt like Dustin Hoffman from the torture scene in *Marathon Man*. Then, the doctor latched on to what felt like my cerebral cortex, braced his foot on the edge of the gurney, and yanked as hard as he could. Like a magician, he started pulling out an endless spool of wadded gauze. Nurses, orderlies, and other patients stared in disbelief as the pile of crusty cotton ballooned to the size of an unwrapped pharaoh.

As I cowered and convalesced on the table, the doctor said, "It's a bit ironic, it was the bandages and not the break that almost killed you."

"What a relief," I thought. "What a relief."

I should have taken up badminton—or become a writer!

Extracurricular Lessons

My freshman year in college, I was assigned two room-mates. One was a fifteen-year-old from Beijing, who was on a full academic scholarship. He was the Asian version of Doogie Howser. His sole possessions included a small backpack containing a single change of clothes, a Casio watch with a built-in calculator, and a first edition copy of *The Double Helix: A Personal Account of the Discovery of the Structure of DNA* by Dr. James D. Watson. My other room-mate was the sheltered only child of a wealthy New York socialite. His name was Augustus, and he looked like he could have been the cover model for the classic 1980 field guide, *The Official Preppy Handbook*. Augustus had never been away from home, so, for the first week and a half, he simply lay in bed whimpering like an abandoned puppy.

The two caused me to seriously question the validity of the roommate placement survey I had filled out over the summer.

Fortunately, I had a wrestling teammate who was in a similar predicament. Chuck's assigned roommate was a self-proclaimed geek—long before it was popular to make such a proclamation, I might add. When he wasn't study-ing computer science on Science Drive, he could be found cloistered in the school's dungeon-like video arcade play-

With my
roommate
Chuck and
his Barracuda
at Duke
University, ca.
1985

Being rescued by
my roommate
Chuck, ca. 1985

ing Space Invaders, Ms. Pac-Man, or Galaga.

Chuck and I quickly arranged for a trade.

Charles (Chuck) Egerton was from Baltimore. At 142, he was only one weight class above me, but he was built like a Sherman tank. He looked like a slightly smaller version of Dwayne "The Rock" Johnson. Though we were already well into the 80s, Chuck was firmly ensconced in the 70s. He wore terrycloth shirts with huge collars and designer jeans, he listened to Rush, The Eagles, Queen, and Lynyrd Skynyrd, he collected Lava Lamps and black light posters, and he drove a puke-green Plymouth Barracuda with white racing stripes.

As I would soon discover, Chuck was also an extremely successful Lothario. Because of this, I spent much of my freshman year sleeping on a couch in the common room. Needless to say, the arrangement was not exactly conducive to good study habits. It made for a tough year.

I learned a valuable lesson though: solutions, especially those that seem obvious at the time, can actually cause their own problems. It was the first of many extracurricular lessons I would discern far, far from the classroom. The following are just a few of the others:

A Close Shave

I was a short-order cook at a college bar. We served hamburgers, hoagies, cheese fries, and onion rings. Late one night, I got slammed with a huge order of cheeseburgers. I threw a few patties on the grill and buttered some buns—everything tastes better with butter -, before I realized that we were out of cheese. I ducked into the walk-in freezer, grabbed a huge block of cheddar, and started cutting it on the large, stainless steel industrial slicer. Every time I slid the block over the spinning blade, it made the sound, "Sha-shunk. Sha-shunk, sha-shunk, sha-shunk…"

Watching the patties on the grill and listening to the soothing sound of the slicer, I thought about the biology test I had the next day, an upcoming wrestling match against Clemson, and a cute girl I had met the night before at a sorority party. Then, I heard a different sound. It was an abrupt and disturbing, "Ka-Chunk!" I felt a sharp pang in my right hand. I fired off a bevy of expletives and turned toward the machine, where I saw a geyser of what I had hoped was ketchup spurting up high into the air. If I were describing the accident today (which I am), I would definitely reference the derrick scene from the aptly titled film, *There Will Be Blood*.

Without looking at what was surely a gruesome wound, I lunged for my mangled hand and quickly wrapped it up in reams and reams of paper towels.

"Apply pressure!" ordered the barback as she burst into the kitchen.

Sensing my apprehension, she added in a voice like Ally McBeal's, "Don't worry, I'm pre-med."

Inspecting the floor and not my hand, she said, "You've obviously lost a great deal of blood. You'll definitely need a tourniquet." She pulled out a dirty dishtowel from her apron and tied it tightly around my wrist. "If we hope to save the severed digit," she continued, "you'll need to keep it on ice." She filled a plastic bag with cubes from the well and attached it to my hand with an entire roll of Saran Wrap. "Now, get to the hospital," she said!

Pleased with her triage, the barback returned to the floor to retrieve empty beer bottles and soiled paper plates.

With my cocooned hand in tow, I jumped into my manager's Dodge Dart and we raced—about as much as you can possibly "race" in a Dodge Dart—toward the Duke University Medical Center.

On the way over, I pleaded with my boss, an eleventh-year senior, "We have to save my finger! If we don't, I'll never play guitar again!"

"But you don't play guitar," my manager pointed out.

"Yes, but I plan to learn," I said.

"Jerry Garcia's missing a finger," he said. "And so is Mac Rebennack, better known as Dr. John. They seem to do just fine."

"Good point," I said, "but I'd still like to keep the finger."

When we arrived at the hospital, I ran into the Emergency Room screaming, well, "bloody murder!" I pushed past a man having a heart attack, I cut in front of a woman who had been in a terrible automobile accident, and I barked at a guy who I'm pretty sure later became a homicide victim.

"Doctor, doctor," I screamed!

"Gimme the news," chimed in my manager, "I got a bad case of lovin' you!"

"Not funny," I said. "I may have lost my finger—or possibly even my entire hand! Please doctor, do what you can to save it!"

"Well, let's take a look," he said. The ER doctor pulled out a pair of scissors the size of garden shears and starting cutting away at my makeshift bandages.

A small crowd had gathered around like rubberneck-

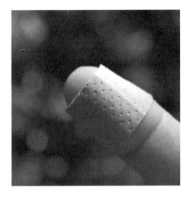

ers eager to witness the sure-to-be hideous carnage within.

When the doctor finally reached my hand, there was a collective sigh of disappointment from the crowd. They looked like trick-or-treaters who had just been given a box of old crusty raisins.

The small wound on the tip of my right index finger was the size of a single hole-punched paper chad. The missing skin was about the width of, well, a thin slice of sharp cheddar cheese.

"If you would like," said the doctor, "I could give you a Band-Aid."

"No, that's ok," I said with air of stoicism. "It's just a flesh wound."

During my biology test the next morning, I remember scribbling in the margins of my blue examination book, "Know the facts before you (over)react."

They Call Him the Streak

Myrtle Beach is considered the miniature golf capital of the Western Hemisphere. According to a somewhat reliable source, there are more putt-putt courses there than anywhere else on the planet. Its water tower is actually shaped like a giant golf ball. It's also a popular Spring Break destination for the students of Duke University. In

1988, I drove down with Chuck in the aforementioned Plymouth Barracuda.

Because I was rooming with the Terrycloth Casanova, I didn't spend much time in my motel room. Instead, I hung out (and sometimes slept) on the beach or in the lobby.

One afternoon, I walked into my "inside" bedroom and found eight guys huddled together on the floor. They were debating what to do next. Apparently, there was still plenty of time between being hung over and toasting Happy Hour.

"What about streaking." one of them suggested.

"Yeah, streaking, that sounds cool," another responded.

They then looked over at me as though I were the one potential dissenting vote on the Supreme Court. "Sure," I acquiesced, "why not."

In retrospect, of course there were plenty of reasons "why not." But, because we had obviously left our common sense in Durham, North Carolina, we ignored them all.

We disrobed and took off (I know, a bit redundant) down the beach.

As we did, we sang the famous song by Ray Stevens, "The Streak." "Oh, yes, they call him the Streak / Look at that, look at that / Fastest thing on two feet / Look at that, look at that!"

And, "look at that" they did! There were catcalls and laughter from the college crowd, and there were shrieks and angry taunts from retirees, parents, and kids.

Soon, there were also sirens blaring on the main drag. And, a growing posse of policemen, security guards, lifeguards, protective dads, and "good" Samaritans gathered on the dunes.

"Who ARE those guys?" I asked in my best Paul Newman voice.

"Hopefully, not the Bolivian army," answered a friend who obviously got the reference.

Within minutes, we were completely surrounded. We were like the British at Dunkirk, only without Winston Churchill rallying support on the mainland. Prospects of escape (or a major motion picture recounting our heroic and desperate exploits) seemed grim.

I figured we had three options: 1) We could run into the surf and swim to the nearest island. Unfortunately, the nearest island was Bermuda, which was 842 miles away. Assuming we couldn't make the crossing, we would be forced to come out of the cold Atlantic water and face both capture and humiliation. 2) We could stay the course. Like the British athletes from *Chariots of Fire*, we could outrun our adversaries to an inspirational score by Vangelis Papathanassiou. Depending on our trajectory, we wouldn't stop until we reached either Wilmington or Charleston. Or 3) We would charge directly into the gauntlet like the famed 300 at the Battle of Thermopylae, only with fewer cloths, no weapons, and little courage.

To pull off any one of these options would have required leadership, communication, and coordination— unfortunately, three additional things we sorely lacked.

Instead, we scattered like frightened fiddler crabs.

I ran directly toward a guy who looked like the East Coast version of David Hasselhoff. As I did, I had flashbacks from my grade school days playing flag football, only this time, my solitary flag was tenuously attached to my body and not a flimsy belt! The stakes were considerably higher!

I made a move like the Heisman trophy statue, with my right hand clutching something other than a football, and The Hoff crashed into the sand. I then averted one tackle after another, before darting into the back entrance of a beach-side hotel. As I crossed the lobby, the concierge threw a stack of brochures at me, and a bellboy tried to trip me with a Samsonite suitcase.

"Safely" outside, I crossed a busy intersection to the sound of blasting horns and screeching brakes. On the other side of the street, I entered an eighteen-hole putt-putt golf course. (Did I mention that Myrtle Beach has putt-putt courses?) As I darted across the tiny greens, young children snickered and angry parents threatened me with putting irons. At the back side of the course, there was a tall chain-link fence with a row of sharp prongs across the top. I hesitated like a mother penguin about to jump off a glacier into water boiling with both krill and leopard seals. I then scaled the fence, gingerly threw my legs over the top, leapt to the ground, and, immediately checked to make sure that all body parts were accounted for. Thankfully, they were.

Like Sherman in reverse, I continued my march *away from* the sea. I ran through two residential neighborhoods, past a church, a school, a fire station, and a strip mall. Eventually, I entered a large wooded park. There, I discovered a public bathroom with an open broom closet to hide in.

Naked and afraid—long before I could make money for it on a reality TV show—I waited in the dark closet for the sun to finally set.

When it did, I fashioned shorts from a black plastic garbage bag, and slowly plodded my way back to our motel.

Of the nine guys who had gone streaking that day, only three returned. The other six had been arrested and fined for indecent exposure and resisting arrest. Author's Note: Based on terrifying testimonials from our imprisoned colleagues, it is definitely not advisable to resist arrest while naked!

After the three of us recounted our "Great Escapes," one of them proclaimed, "Ok, that's the last time I do mushrooms!"

"Mushrooms?" I asked.

"Yeah, we should never have eaten those &%$#ing 'shrooms," he said.

"True," I lied.

On the beach the next day, wearing a bathing suit, a tee-shirt, sunglasses, and a hat, I thought to myself, "Groupthink, especially when influenced by hallucinogenic fungi, often results in poor decision-making."

Cat on a Hot Dorm Roof

My friend Bill had just pulled three consecutive all-nighters preparing for final exams. After his last test on Friday, he went to his room, closed all the shades, cranked up the AC, and buried himself beneath a mountain of dirty sheets, blankets, and clothes. His plan was to hibernate until Monday.

Unfortunately for Bill, his hall mates and I had other plans.

We waited until he reached REM (not that long), and then tossed a gross of bottle rockets into his cave-like room. We closed the door and broke down laughing pre(im)maturely.

Needless to say, it was a rude awakening.

The room lit up like a lighthouse. An explosion of fireworks was followed by an explosion of expletives. Bill was as angry as a pig being castrated. He launched himself at us like, well, that same unhappy swine. Author's note: I once had the extreme displeasure of castrating a boar. It was (or at least it seemed at the time) as uncomfortable for me as it was for him. In retrospect, it probably wasn't.

When he finally calmed down (sort of), we cleaned up the confetti from the pyrotechnics, and we pleaded our juvenile case: "Exams are over dude! It's time to celebrate. The main quad is gonna be insane. Every fraternity and sorority is throwing a party tonight. We HAVE to go!"

Bill yawned, wacked me upside the head with a study guide, and said, "OK, I'm in."

As we skipped toward the campus festivities, I looked back over my shoulder and saw smoke trickling out of Bill's third floor window. "Holy @#$%!," I yelled! "The dorm's on fire!"

"Holy @#$%!," screamed Bill, "RUN!"

"Run?" I said, "But what about Wing-Nut?"

Wing-nut was my cat. I called her "Wing-nut" because she had an abnormally tiny head and huge, bat-like ears.

"Wing-nut's a &%$# cat," said Bill. "She'll be fine. We're the ones who are in trouble. I'm gonna lose my &%$# scholarship. Let the dorm master take care of the fire. We'll hide out until the smoke clears. If anybody asks, we'll blame it on those douchebags from ΣAE. Or, better yet, UNC!"

"No," I protested, "I gotta save the Nut."

So, as my classmates fled into the Duke Forest like Harrison Ford in *The Fugitive*, I ran toward the burning building like Steve McQueen in *Towering Inferno*.

I bounded up the stairs, sounded the fire alarm, and burst into the smoke-filled hallway on the third floor. I grabbed a fire extinguisher off the wall and emptied it into Bill's smoldering room. I then carefully disposed of any potential incriminating evidence, and began searching for my frightened cat, Wing-nut.

A few minutes later, the fire department arrived.

Covered in retardant and coughing from the smoke, I declared, "Stand down gentleman—there's no need to worry. I have everything under control. I evacuated the dorm and put out the fire. I'm pretty sure bad wiring on an old lava lamp was the culprit. Everybody is safe and accounted for. Everybody that is, except our dorm mascot, Wing-nut. She's a beautiful feline with a small head, big ears, and a long tail. She must have gotten spooked by the smoke and alarm."

At that moment, we heard a faint cry outside an open window. Apparently, Wing-nut had climbed up on the roof. "You guys wouldn't happen to have a long ladder?" I asked.

Later that night, I got a meeting request from the Dean of Students. "She probably wants to thank me for saving the dorm," I told a friend. "Or, perhaps, she wants to give me a medal or mention me during the upcoming commencement ceremony. I'll surely be heralded as a hero!"

But, alas, that was not the case.

When I met with the dean the following day, she asked, "So, Mr. Dunbar, you do realize that cats are not allowed in the dorms?"

"Um, a, uh, no ma'am," I stammered.

"The cat has to go immediately," she said. "And, I want the lava lamps gone as well. The dorm rooms already have adequate (and safe) lighting. And, finally, you'll need to reimburse the university for the cost of retrieving your cat from the roof. The Durham Fire Department doesn't work for us."

The next day, as I cut a rubber check to the university, I thought to myself, "It's probably not a good idea to jump into the spotlight—when you have something to hide."

Petuahua

Duke University's Phi Kappa Alpha fraternity's end-of-year soirée was called Petuahua. It was basically a Polynesian version of the toga party in *Animal House*. There were tropical drinks, grass skirts and leis, a water slide, a grotto, and an "active" volcano.

My junior year, I was asked to choreograph the culminating hula. Though I lacked the credentials, in both experience and ability, I leapt at the opportunity like a ballerina in *Swan Lake*.

I envisioned a combination of a Mardi Gras flambeaux and a Maori haka, with a little Martha Graham thrown in for good measure.

My plan was for us to emerge from the woods like a band of wild savages chanting "Petua-hua" (think of the opening scene from *Raiders of the Lost Ark*), run through the crowd, circle around several dorms, retrieve a stash of hidden tiki torches, enter a large culvert, and then reemerge in front of the crowd via a storm drain (think

Recovering from a college party at Duke University, ca. 1988

Simón Bolívar's heroic maneuvering to reach Boyacá). We would then perform an elaborate and boisterous haka (think the 610 Stompers from New Orleans in Polynesian garb). For our grand finale, we would plunge down the waterslide and hurl our lit torches into the volcano, causing it to erupt (think of the opening ceremony at the Olympics, if it were held on the Big Island of Hawaii that is). In retrospect, my plan may have been a tad bit too ambitious.

Before the show, my troupe and I did Mai Tai shots from hollowed out coconut shells. Author's note: As most people know, the coconut is the largest nut in the world. Considering our un-dance-worthy condition after the libation, we probably should have used something smaller, say a macadamia nut.

Wearing nothing but body paint, a makeshift loincloth, and a pair of Cole Haan driving loafers, I led my inebriated crew through the crowd chanting something utterly unintelligible. As we approached the dorms, I decided to take a shortcut through what I thought was an open window. As it turns out, it was actually just uncharacteristically clean. I crashed through the window and landed in a heap on a carpet of shattered glass. I quickly checked beneath my loincloth, brushed off the glass, hopped to my feet, and beckoned my fellow dancers to follow. But, instead, they simply opened the door and waltzed in.

As we ran through the building, I heard a sloshing sound coming from my right Cole Haan driving loafer. "Maybe I stepped in a puddle," I thought.

"But why would there be a puddle in the middle of a dorm?" I reasoned. I then looked down and saw a bloody iceberg jutting up through the top of my shoe.

Stating the obvious, a friend pointed at my impaled foot and screamed, "Holy &%$# dude, that's gotta hurt?!"

"Strangely, it doesn't," I slurred. "The Mai Tais are working like morphine."

"Enough to dance?" he asked.

"No, probably not," I admitted. "Y'all are gonna have to perform without me."

Then, like William B. Travis in old San Antonio, I delivered a rousing speech to my obviously disheartened crew. "Victory or death!" I proclaimed at the end. "The show MUST go on!"

I then climbed up on a friend's back, and we trotted off toward the Duke University Medical Center.

When I arrived at the emergency room, a nurse put

me in a wheelchair and handed me one of those flimsy gowns that opens up in the back. But, then she rescinded the offer. "You're uncovered (and humiliated) enough," she said. "The loincloth will do just fine."

When the doctor arrived, he asked with a wry smile, "Weren't you the patient with the missing finger?"

"Yep, that was me," I confessed. "It's healed up nicely, don't you think?"

"You must have had a good doctor," he said.

"Yes," I said. "He didn't even leave a scar."

"This seems to be a bit more serious," said the doctor. "I think it might require more than a Band-Aid."

He removed the shard with a pair of metal tongs and probed the wound with gloved fingers. "It's a miracle you didn't tear any muscles or ligaments," he said. "The glass went straight through."

As he stitched up my foot, he added, "When the local anesthesia and alcohol wear off, you're gonna be in a world of pain. Stay here while I write you a prescription."

As I was waiting for the doctor to return, there was a sudden flurry of activity in the hospital. It was like a M*A*S*H unit during the Battle of Heartbreak Ridge. Apparently, a waterslide on campus had collapsed. There had also been an unusual volcanic eruption that was said to have rivaled that of Krakatoa. Windows had shattered throughout campus, and the explosion was heard as far away as Chapel Hill.

In the midst of the melee, an announcement was made over the intercom: "The Dean of Students at the university would like for all students injured on campus tonight to be held until tomorrow." It sounded rather ominous.

I arched my eyebrows like Jack Nickolson in *One Flew Over the Cuckoo's Nest* (before the frontal lobotomy that is), and declared, "%$#@ that!" I commandeered a wheelchair and hastily headed toward the exit. As I wheeled my way down the hallway, orderlies screamed and patients cheered. At the emergency room entrance, I jumped out of the chair and sprinted toward campus on my stitched-up foot.

Back in the ruins of our dorm, I threw back a Mai Tai, curled up on a couch and passed out.

I woke up the next morning reeling in pain. I felt like a coyote whose foot had been crushed in an iron trap. (At one point, I actually considered gnawing it off.) It was then that I thought to myself, "Ya gotta look before you leap. And, you should probably think before you run."

The Bicycle Diaries
Misadventures on Two Wheels

Keeping it Cool in Key West

In my early teens, like a lot of kids in their early teens, I had an unfledged sense of what was "cool." Unlike my dad who had grown up with Cary Grant and Humphrey Bogart, I had been (regrettably) influenced by the likes of Fonzie, Gallagher, and Mork. I wore brightly colored suspenders with baggy army fatigues, I rolled up one pant leg and the opposite shirtsleeve, I had a blonde streak in my hair inspired by Mel Gibson in *Mad Max*, and I juggled disparate objects while riding a unicycle. I also liked to rattle off animal fun-facts in the voice of my hero, Sir David Attenborough. (Come to think of it, I still do that.)

On a family trip to Key West, Florida, I met a girl named Lilly. Lilly was as cute as a baby marmoset, was single, and, most importantly, was younger than me, i.e., impressionable.

So, I did my best to, well, impress her. I wore my Che Guevera black beret with a red star, I quoted lines from *Monty Python and the Holy Grail*, and I blathered *fun* facts about the local fauna, including the Key deer, Florida panther, and American crocodile. Sadly, but not surprisingly, Lilly was not impressed.

Still wearing suspenders
in college

On a bicycle tour
of town, I came up
with a new, foolproof
plan: I would show
off my musical tal-
ents by drumming
Beatles tunes on the
hoods and roofs of
parked cars. I would
serenade Lilly with
"Can't Buy Me
Love," "Eight Days a
Week," and "Love Me Do." During the ride, she would
surely fall in love with me like Barbara Bach with Ringo
Starr on the set of *Caveman*.

But alas, it was not to be. While focusing on my drumming, I failed to adjust my steering to accommodate the
occasional wider vehicle. During a rather spirited rendition of "Get Back," my knee crashed into the bumper of a
white Chevrolet van. I collapsed on the pavement, curled
up like a pill bug, and howled "Helter Skelter" in agony.

Lilly swerved into traffic in order to miss me, stopped
and, to my dismay, came back to see if I was OK.

I was not.

Like the final chord from "A Day in the Life," my bicycle tour (and potential date) had come to an abrupt and
dramatic end.

For the rest of the trip, I searched (unsuccessfully) for

sunken pirate treasure. I tied a large magnet to a long rope and dragged it through the shallows. "Surely," I thought, "Lilly would find this cool."

Le Tour de Campus

Duke University in Durham, North Carolina, is split into two campuses, East and West. I lived in the East, but took classes in the West. Every day, I would ride the 1.8 miles between the two on my Trek mountain bike.

During my commute, I would often race the university shuttle bus. Over time, a heated rivalry developed between the driver and me. We became the Fausto Coppi and the Gino Bartali of the Piedmont.

For me, Fausto, the key to victory was the traffic light at the midway point. If it was red, the bus had to stop, but I didn't. I'd run the light, pick up a substantial lead, and cruise to the finish line, a statue of James B. Duke, the tobacco baron who had founded the university. If the light was green though, it was a different story; it was anybody's race.

On the Friday before summer break, the final stage of *Le Tour de Campus*, the bus and I left East Campus in an all-out sprint. For the first three-quarters of a mile, the lead changed several times.

As we approached the traffic light though, I saw a yellow glow, and I beamed with confidence. I glared over at the passengers and raised my arms in triumph like Lance Armstrong on the Champs-Élysées—until, that is, my chin slammed into the bus's large rectangular side-view mirror. There was a loud "Crack!" I flew backwards, while my bike, still in the race, continued on without me. It sailed through the intersection, wobbled up a steep hill,

The author mountain biking in Idaho in 2017

careened off the side of the road, flipped over the curb, and landed in a bush.

The bus driver took an obligatory glance down at me to make sure that I was still alive, flashed a crooked smile, raised a solitary finger, and stepped on the gas. As he pulled away, he waved a yellow jersey out the window — and the passengers all cheered.

(not) **Breaking Away**

There was a basketball game that night, so I had the William R. Perkins Library all to myself.

I ran the stacks like a bibliophile on speed. I found a first edition of Edward Gibbon's *The History of the Decline and Fall of the Roman Empire* and a leather-bound copy of *La Relación* by Cabeza de Vaco. I was in history geek nirvana!

When the librarian finally kicked me out, it was almost midnight. The game had ended, and the main quad was all but empty.

The library is next to the Chapel, which is located at the top of a long drive ending in a turnaround. Like the brakeman on a bobsled, I liked to build up a good head of steam for the run down Chapel Drive.

I rolled up my right pant leg, slung my backpack over my shoulder (in a manner that was cool but definitely not safe), and, because it was cold, tucked my hands inside my sweatshirt sleeves. I jumped on my bike and took off like Dennis Christopher in *Breaking Away*.

As I approached the turnaround, I was going so fast, my eyes began to water. Through the tears, and at the last possible second, I saw a chain stretched across the street. Apparently, the turnaround was closed to traffic (and me).

In the split second that remained, I envisioned three scenarios: 1) like Ponch in that famous episode from CHiPs, I could slide beneath the chain and pop up on the other side, 2) like Evel Knievel on his Harley-Davidson XR-750, I could jump over it or 3) like a Cirque Du Soleil acrobat, I could do some gravity-defying combination of the two, and land on the moving saddle in a handstand. Unfortunately, none of these scenarios came to pass. I simply hit the chain.

The front tire collapsed like an accordion, and I sailed over the handlebars. I flew through the air for about twenty yards, and then tumbled across the pavement for another twenty.

When I finally came to a bloody halt, I figured the worst was over. Then, I heard a whistling sound above my head. Like Wile E. Coyote, I looked up just in time to be struck in the face by the crumpled remains of my broken bicycle.

Hearing the commotion, hundreds of students streamed out of dorm rooms and frat houses all across campus. It was as if Duke had just beaten North Carolina in the NCAA finals. Author's note: When they saw my asphalt-flayed body, many of the students screamed and ran back to their rooms.

Fortunately for me, the Medical Center was nearby.

The next day, the school newspaper, *The Chronicle*, ran a headline on page three that read, "Sophomore Survives Epic Crash."

From my hospital gurney, I added, "Just barely."

Missing the Exit for Uscita

And Learning a Valuable Lesson
about the Importance of Language

I was only three weeks into my Peace Corps training when my host family invited me to a funeral. Funerals are never easy, but this one was particularly awkward. I didn't know anyone, and my Spanish at the time was *muy mal*. Mourners were saying things like, "He was such a kind and honest man; he was a gentle and loving father; and he represented the very best of our unique Andean culture." I wanted to contribute something, but I didn't know what to say or even how to say it. I racked my brain for an appropriate condolence. Finally, I came up with the generic, "¡*Qué pena!*" or "What a pity!" Instead though, I blurted out, "¡*Qué pene!*" I was only off by a letter, but it made a world of difference. I said, "Yeah, and he had a huge penis!" The somber procession erupted into raucous laughter.

Two years earlier, I had had a similar experience—an experience that also taught me a valuable lesson about the importance of language.

My junior year in college, I spent a semester abroad. I was a history major, and my dream was to study in Rome. I wanted to walk in the footsteps of Julius Caesar, Marcus Aurelius, and Constantine the Great; read Virgil, Catu-

Looking for directions in Italy

lus, and Ovid from the famed Seven Hills; race around the Circus Maximus like Charlton Heston in *Ben Hur*; and stammer like *I, Claudius* in the sibyl's cave.

So, I took off a semester, took on a few extra jobs, and saved up enough money for the trip. Unfortunately, when I arrived in Italy, the dollar collapsed against the lira like the Roman Empire to the barbarians. I ended up living off plain pasta and boxed Frascati. So much for bread and circuses!

In the morning, I studied ancient history, architecture, and art. In the afternoon, there were classes in Italian and Greek, but I skipped those. I figured six months wasn't long enough to learn a new language. And besides, "When in Rome…."

One weekend, I squirreled together enough cash to join friends on a quick excursion to Florence. We'd check out the Uffizi, gawk at Michelangelo's David, and drink

Lambrusco on the Ponte Vecchio. We left on Friday. By Sunday, I was as broke as a plebian. I couldn't afford another night at the hostel, so I spent the rest of my lire on a train ticket back to Rome. My friends would return the following morning.

As the train left the station, a porter came by to punch my ticket. I then closed my eyes and went to sleep.

When the train came to a stop, I looked out the window and saw a sign that read, "Uscita." I didn't know the town, but I assumed it was on the way to Rome. I thought I had taken the express train, but apparently, I hadn't. I closed my eyes and went back to sleep.

A few minutes later, the porter woke me up to stamp my ticket again. When I handed it to him, he said, "Scusami, Roma was a backa der." He pointed over his shoulder.

"That was Uscita," I corrected him.

"No, uscita meansa exit," he said in broken English. "We now a go to Napoli. It a costa mora lira."

"*My dispach*," I said, "but I don't have *mora* lira."

"It's mi dispiace," he corrected me. "Come a dis away." The porter escorted me to a detention car at the back of the train. In Naples, he transferred me to a proper "debtors' prison" in the station. I was thrown into a cell with about ten other deadbeat travelers.

"Trying to make light of the situation, I turned to my fellow inmates and declared, "I'm Spartacus!" To my surprise, no one repeated the line. They obviously hadn't seen the classic film by Stanley Kubrick. I then tried a bit from *The Life of Brian*, and asked, "What did the Romans ever do for us?!" After a long uncomfortable pause, I said, "All right, but apart from the sanitation, the medicine, education, wine, public order, irrigation, roads, the fresh-water system, and public health, what have the Romans ever *really* done for us?" Again, there was nothing but crickets!

An old man, obviously feeling sorry for me (and my disastrous comedy routine), handed me a loaf of stale bread and some hard cheese. "Grazie," I said. I then quipped, "This is no *dolce vita?*!" The old man just shook his head.

Over the next two hours, I plotted my escape. Like Steve McQueen in *Papillon* or Tim Robbins in *The Shawshank Redemption*, I was determined to win my freedom! I asked the "warden" if I could use the bathroom. There, I discovered a tiny window used for ventilation. I knocked out the frame and squeezed through the hole. On the outside, I ran for a train heading in the other direction and hopped on like a hobo. (Hopefully all tracks, like all roads, led to Rome?) I ducked into a bathroom, locked the door and sat on the toilet. Whenever anyone knocked, I grunted and heaved like a hippopotamus in heat. When the train stopped, I bolted out the door and ran like the fugitive that I was.

I then hopped on a bus heading toward the university. At the next stop, an inspector got on, something that rarely happens in Rome. I took out my monthly pass, only to discover that it had expired about five hours earlier. He kicked me off.

Walking along the Tiber as the sun slowly climbed over the Seven Hills, I thought to myself, "This was no *Roman &%#@ Holiday*!"

When I finally arrived at the dorm, my roommate was already back from Florence. "What the hell happened to you?" he asked.

"I missed the exit for Uscita," I confessed.

"That's *molto brutto*," he said.

"Sì," I said.

That afternoon I sat in on my first class of *Italian for Beginners*.

Fight-or-Flight
A Few Noteworthy Encounters with other Species

The Rooster

One of my first chores as a child was gathering the eggs. My brother and sister called me "The Eggman, Coo Coo Cachoo." Every afternoon, I would walk back to the barn and raid nests in three large chicken coops. The first two were easy, but the third was a different story…

The year before we had gone to the State Fair in Hammond, Louisiana. They had a game where you had to pitch a nickel into a glass jar. It looked easy, but, like most arcade games, it wasn't. We spent hours (and probably a mint) tossing coins. Finally, while we weren't looking, my father slipped the man a ten-dollar bill and the man handed me a chick. Unbeknownst to us, the adorable chick was actually a dude. He grew up to be one of the biggest and meanest roosters we ever had. We called him Goblin.

Goblin ruled the third coop like a North Korean dictator. He was cruel and ruthless. Whenever I entered the pen, he puffed up his chest, flashed his long-curved spurs, and squawked in protest.

One day while I was hunched over picking up eggs, Goblin crept up behind me as stealthily as a panther and pounced on my back. He thrust a spur deep into my side

and pecked violent-
ly at the back of my
neck. He had obvious-
ly had enough of me
stealing his progeny!

After an epic battle
filled with blood, tears,
and feathers, I finally
freed myself from the
tyrannical fowl. An-
gry and embarrassed,
I picked up a broken
rake handle and flung it at the bird. It spun across the coop
like a boomerang, striking Goblin in his long cocky neck.
He dropped like a sack of chicken feed. Our prized (and
expensive) state fair rooster was dead and gone.

To this day, my family holds it against me. After every
dispute, they remind me, "Yeah, but you killed Goblin!"

"Yes," I say. "I know."

The Deer

I went to visit a farmer in Zhumar, Ecuador. He was
attempting to raise rainbow trout in earthen ponds. At
the time, I was a Peace Corps volunteer and worked with
small animals, including fish.

When I arrived, the farmer was nowhere to be found.
Apparently, he was out trying to round up a fugitive cow.

The farmer had a pet deer he had raised from a fawn.
It was tethered to a wooden stake near one of the ponds.
Curious, I walked up to the animal and pressed a hand

against its antlers. It instinctively pushed back. I pressed again and the buck reared up to butt me, but the rope held him at bay. I then pressed (my luck) a third time. The deer dug in with his hoofs and lunged with all his might, ripping the stake from the ground. Like that old poster of a locomotive going off a bridge, I simply said, "Oh shit!"

I tried to run away, but the deer, well, ran like a deer. He quickly overtook me and knocked me down. He swung his head from side to side like a medieval mace. I covered my head with my hands and curled up on the ground like a frightened pangolin. The deer reared up on his hind legs for one last, decisive, and fatal blow. He came down with his mighty rack and drove a point through my jeans and into my butt. I let out a bloodcurdling scream and dove headlong for one of the trout ponds.

About a half an hour later, when the farmer finally came to my rescue, I was still cowering in the cold muddy water—with an extra hole in my derrière.

The Bees

Abejas, or bees, were my biggest failure as a Peace Corps volunteer. I kept a couple of hives at my site in Zhamar, Ecuador, and tried in vain to convince the locals to do the same. It was a tough sell. The Africanized or "killer" bees were aggressive, and honey wasn't exactly a hot commodity in the high Andes.

One day, a friend and neighbor of mine appeared at my door. His name was Guillermo. He was sixteen and one of the few people in the entire *paróquia* of Jima who had any interest whatsoever in abejas. He told me there was a swarm down by the river and asked me if I could catch it. "*¡Por supuesto!*" I said, "Of course! And you can keep the hive." This was the turning point I had been waiting for.

We put on our gear and headed down to the Rio Moya. The swarm was on the side of a cliff about forty feet above the water. The plan was for Guillermo to placate the bees with smoke while I isolated the queen. Less than a minute into the operation though, Guillermo started tapping me on the shoulder. "*Estoy ocupado*, I'm busy," I said. He tapped even harder. I turned around and saw that his veil was filled with angry bees! He shrieked in horror as we both tumbled down the side of the ravine.

The next day was Sunday, *El Dia de Mercado* or market day. Everyone was there, including Guillermo. His head was the size of a beach ball and it was covered in blistering welts. From that point forward, there would be no beekeeping in Jima! It wasn't exactly the turning point I had hoped for.

The Mice

"Folwell, I've got a problem." Ms. Bailey, one of the kindergarten teachers, was definitely in a panic. She looked around my room to make sure there were no children and closed the door. "As you know," she said, "our classroom pets are two mice, Mickey and Minnie. Well, apparently, they decided to start a family. Now we've got eight! Can you help me out?"

"Of course," I said. "Just tell the kids you donated them to the zoo."

Our eight-grade mascots were two speckled king snakes

named Salt and Pepper. They LOVED mice.

The next day, I turned down the lights, turned up Richard Wagner's "Ride of the Valkyries," and dropped the six pinkies into the terrarium. The kids shrieked as the snakes inhaled their breakfast. A few minutes later, the happy reptiles were basking on a heated rock and we were discussing FDR's New Deal.

I figured that was the end of it.

It wasn't.

Schools, regardless of their size, are small places. And kids, like adults, talk.

The eruption from the kindergarten wing rivaled that of Vesuvius in AD 79. There were deafening howls and buckets of tears. At one-point, things got so bad the principal actually considered calling in a crisis team.

Almost twenty years later, I ran into one of Ms. (now Mrs.) Bailey's students. The first thing she said was, "Mr. Dunbar, I still haven't forgiven you!"

"Yes," I said. "I know."

I guess it's true what they say: "All you really need to know, you probably learned in kindergarten."

The Ants

I was playing in a Whiffle Ball tournament with friends at Wisner Center Park off Tchoupitoulas Street in New Orleans. It was the last inning of a close game.

We were down by one with two outs. Like a diminutive version of the mighty Casey, I was at bat.

The first pitch was a curveball (Is there any other kind in whiffle ball?). I swung and missed. The second dropped just before it reached the plate. Strike two. The third pitch hooked to the left as it approached. I lunged and cracked a forehand like Roger Federer. The plastic ball arched out into centerfield. I took off like Pete Rose on a bet. As I was rounding third, the shortstop threw the ball to the catcher. My friend Larry Shoemaker now stood between me and home plate. I was trapped in a pickle.

With the game on the line, my fight-or-flight response kicked in. I looked down in desperation and saw a pile of red ants. In one fell swoop, I scooped up the entire pile and threw it on my (former) friend Larry. Larry screamed in horror, dropped the whiffle ball, and started flailing like a man on fire. I trotted triumphantly across home plate.

No, I'm not proud; but yes, I did hit a homerun in Whiffle Ball!

The Snake

It was one of the first dates with my future wife. I took her and a couple of friends on a boat ride up Bayou Bonfouca near the town of Slidell. At the mouth of a small slough, we saw a family of nutria dining on marsh grass. "That's an invasive species from South America," I said with an arched brow. "You know they're devouring our state's fragile wetlands."

Wanting to prove that I was a man of action, I hopped out of the boat like the Crocodile Hunter and chased after

Fishing for gar in the marshes and swamps near my home, ca. 1987

the aquatic rodents. I knew I couldn't catch them, but I figured my date would be mightily impressed.

I plodded along the edge of the slough as it wound its way deep into the marsh. Nearing the end, I decided to cross over and double back. The slough was narrow at that point; it would be an easy jump—or so I thought. As I pushed off, my feet stuck in the spongy soil and I dropped like a brick, landing face down in soupy mud. So much for impressing my date!

As I lifted my head from the muck, I saw two glistening fangs pointed at my jugular. There was a huge water moccasin coiled up next to my face. It was as thick as an automobile tire and smelled like a corpse. It rattled its tail, cocked its diamond-shaped head, and flashed its cottonmouth. As a millennial might say, "I was in a hot mess!"

The snake, obviously upset that I had interrupted its sunbathing, lunged for my throat. I closed my eyes and shielded myself with the only thing I had, a clod of mud held together with Spartina roots. The snake bit my make-shift shield and stuck like Velcro. It's hooked fangs, like my feet before the fall, were trapped in the mud.

I quickly grabbed the snake behind its head. Not only had I survived, I now had proof of my ordeal. I figured my date would be so impressed with my heroic feat, she would ignore the fact that I was now covered in mud. The live snake was my ace in the hole.

Along the way though, I slipped and fell again. I lost my grip on the snake and landed on top of the angry moccasin. I could feel a hard fang pressed up against my cheek. I rolled over as fast as I could, grabbed the snake by its tail, swung it over my head like a lasso and smashed it against the trunk of a water tupelo. The reptile went limp in my hand; my trump card was lost.

When I arrived back at the boat, my party was an-noyed. They had been waiting in the hot aluminum skiff for more than a half an hour swatting at thirsty mosqui-tos. When I told them my Jack London-like story, they just shook their heads in disbelief. "No, you obviously were embarrassed because you fell in the mud," my date said. "You then found a dead snake and made up a ridiculous story. You should be ashamed of yourself."

To this day, she still doesn't believe me.

The Skunk

I was staying with friends on Avery Island, home of the famous Tabasco pepper sauce. One night, after a few too many adult beverages, we decided to go out and shine animals. The island is teeming with all kinds of cool critters, from black bears and alligators, to banded armadillos and white-tailed deer.

I rode on the roof of an SUV with a spotlight strapped to my head. As we came around a corner, the driver slammed on the brakes. I catapulted over the hood and landed on the dirt road with a "Thud!" Apparently, there was an obstacle in our path. It was *Mephitis mephitis*, better known as a striped skunk. My friends yelled at me to get in the car as they hastily rolled up the windows. Emboldened by alcohol (and a shot of urban stupidity), I refused to yield.

"The little guy is so cute and dainty," I thought, "What harm could it possibly do?" I shook my hands in front of my face and said sarcastically, "Oooooo, I'm so scared!"

The creature pounded its tiny paws on the ground with indignation. "How dare you interfere with my nightly stroll," it seemed to say. Like Pepé Le Pew, it was on a mission to find a mate, and nothing, including me, would stand in its way.

Like the French knight from *Monty Python and the Holy Grail*, I taunted the little creature a second time. "Your mother was a hamster, and your father smelt of elderberry!"

"No," said the skunk. "My parents were skunks and they both smelled far worse! You just pulled my finger pal!"

I had gravely underestimated my foe's formidable defenses. I was Atawalpa to his Pizarro; I was the Japanese at Pearl Harbor: I had just awoken a sleeping giant!

The skunk spun around, did a front handstand, and pinched its butt cheeks together like an old man before a prostate exam. It fired off a powerful and pungent spray. The stream hit me squarely in the face and chest. I winced in horror at the vile stench. It smelled like rancid, musky vinegar, like a fart inside a rotting corpse wrapped in the petals of a blooming titan arum flower.

The skunk had obviously never heard of the Geneva Protocol!

It looked at me as if to say, "I told you so," waved its striped tail like a victory banner and slowly sashayed off into the woods.

Defeated and ashamed, I moped back to the car where I was met with contempt and scowls. My "friends" reluctantly let me in and took me home. There, I marinated for the rest of the night in a huge tub of Tabasco Bloody Mary Mix.

Needless to say, I was not invited back to the island.

To this day, like a Vietnam vet suffering from PTSD, I sometimes catch a faint whiff of that dreadful night—and cringe!

The Spider

I used to bring animals and animal artifacts to schools. I called it "Mr. Dunbar's Featured Creature." Every month, I would "feature" a different group of critters. There were turtles, frogs, and snakes, invasive species, prehistoric fossils, and birds of prey.

Of all the creatures though, arachnids were definitely the most popular. Kids loved the invisible yo-yo trick, the lightning speed of the trapdoor spider, and the macabre story of how the black widow got her name. The star of the show was always the Chilean rose hair tarantula. She brought down the house. On one occasion, literally!

I was in an elementary school "cafetorium" in front of an audience of about hundred fidgety kindergarteners (are there any other kind?). Before the grand finale, I lectured the kids about the importance of not frightening the animal. "She's very sensitive," I

said. "She won't bite unless she's threatened (or wants to subdue a tasty cricket). So, I need for all of you to be very, very brave and stay v-e-r-y, v-e-r-y calm."

Apparently, my lecture failed miserably. When I reached into the terrarium and lifted up the giant spider, my audience went berserk! It was as if I had unleashed Godzilla on Tokyo!

Startled by the commotion, the tarantula sunk its massive fangs into the palm of my hand. The pain was excruciating. Like stones hurled from an atlatl, tears flew from my eyes. I blurted out an expletive that caused the kids (and their teachers) to shriek again in horror. And again, the terrified spider responded in kind!

My class had descended into chaos. It was, as I like to say, "about as organized as a sack of spiders!"

I decided then and there that my next "featured creature" would be a puppy!

Falling for a Challenge
And Landing in a HOT Mess

I'm a sucker for a challenge. Always have been.

When I was just six years old, my brother dared me to climb a giant live oak tree in our backyard. It took a while (and some bayou ingenuity), but I eventually reached the first limb, and then shimmied my way up to the top. Over the next two years, I climbed every tree on the property, from loblolly pines and southern magnolias to swamp maples and tupelo gums. They called me, "The Monkey Boy."

In college, I had a running bet with my wrestling teammate, Chuck. After Saturday matches, we would go out drinking shot-for-shot. At sunrise on Sunday, we would race up and down the entire length of Duke University's Wallace Wade Stadium. The loser had to buy drinks the following week. It was the epitome of burning the candle at both ends.

My friend Zack and I have been challenging each other to feats of courage/stupidity for almost thirty years. We've ventured into the wilderness with nothing but a slingshot and a pocketknife, skitched behind cars on icy roads, scaled the face of tall buildings, trekked across Colombia during the height of the drug wars, and streaked down public beaches. His personal favorite is to stack people on his shoulders; I like to converse solely in limericks.

Whatever we do, the wager is always the same: to admit to the other that you were impressed.

Scrapes, bruises and a few close calls aside, none of these stunts ever resulted in a serious injury—except for one....

When I was in college, I worked as a bartender. One night after my shift, my boss, Steve, challenged me to a jalapeño eating contest. I, of course, jumped on the bet like a jaguar on a capybara.

Steve was a southern version of Tom Selleck's Magnum, P.I. Instead of a Hawaiian shirt, he wore Duck Dynasty camouflage; and, instead of a Ferrari, he drove a Ford F-150. He was big and burly, the kinda guy who probably *enjoyed* eating jalapeños.

But I was a freshman in college, and, like most freshmen in college, I *thought* I knew everything. I figured I could defeat Steve's brawn with a little intellectual dexterity. Like David before Goliath, I devised a simple, knock-out strategy: Instead of biting and chewing the peppers, I would cut them into chunks with a paring knife and swallow the pieces whole. With a little luck, I would avoid the heat and win the bet.

If it hadn't been for Steve's apparent immunity to capsaicin, and some errant pepper juice, I'm pretty sure my plan could have succeeded.

But, it didn't.

Before we started, Steve glared at me through squinted eyes, called me "a punk," and whispered in a gravelly voice, "Go ahead, make my day." Unfortunately for me, the movie reference was devastatingly apropos.

I cut a few peppers and started choking them down like horse pills. Within seconds, beads of sweat sprouted from my forehead and tears welled up in my eyes. My face began to quiver as my lips burst into flames.

I glanced over at Steve and saw him casually nibbling on his second pepper. He lifted up the half-eaten jalapeño, rubbed it slowly around the rim of his mouth, licked his lips, and then flashed a devilish grin.

I was definitely in trouble!

I threw back one more green, flaming Kingsford briquette, coughed it up on the bar, and then, like Roberto Durán, cried out, "*¡No más!*"

I plunged my head into the ice machine, and then started chugging everything from beer to vermouth—anything to extinguish the fire!

After consuming several pints and quarts (the origin of the expression, "mind your p's and q's" by the way), I, not surprisingly, had to use the restroom.

Standing over the urinal on spaghetti legs, still reeling from "the agony of defeat," I felt a slight pang from my nether regions.

I looked down at my hands and noticed, to my extreme dismay, that they were covered in jalapeño juice.

The slight pang spread like napalm dropped from a plane. I collapsed on the bathroom floor, curled up in the fetal position, and howled like a howler monkey.

The pain was indescribable; but hell, pun intended, I'll give it a shot: It felt like my private parts had been flayed with a rusty sawzall blade, wrapped in the tentacles of a Portuguese man o' war, and then held over a colony of driver ants that mistook my mutilated member for the probing tongue of a hungry aardvark. Yep, that's pretty much how it felt.

I wept like a child!

At one point, I actually considered lopping it off like Lorena Bobbitt. I figured it probably didn't work anymore anyway.

An hour and a half later, whimpering on a toilet seat with a sack of ice held to my smoldering crotch, I started contemplating my next bet with Steve. Perhaps it would involve climbing trees, sprinting up stadium stairs, or writing limericks.

Grabbing the Bull by the Horns
Is a Nono

"Ya wanna go to a *toros de pueblo* in Nono?" Kyle asked. "We could get there right quick."

I didn't know what or where he was talking about, but I responded without hesitation, "Sure." During that phase of my life, I was agreeable to a fault.

Kyle William Allan was from West Texas. When he spoke Spanish, he sounded like the actor Sam Elliot pitching Ram trucks for Univision. He was fond of the expression, "right quick," which became his Ecuadorian nickname, well, right quick.

He told me that Nono was a small town just northwest of Quito, the country's capital. It was holding its annual *Toros de Pueblo*, the Latin American version of the running of the bulls, the spectacle popularized in Hemingway's *The Sun Also Rises*.[*]

Kyle and I were only in our second month of Peace Corps training, but we were already going stir crazy. We were in dire need of a diversion. Besides, it was Sunday and we had the day off. What we didn't have, I reminded

---

[*] Here in the Crescent City, we have our own, far safer, version of the running of the bulls. San Fermín in Nueva Orleans features women on rollerblades wearing Viking bullhorns and wielding plastic bats as they chase enamored men up and down the streets. "Tora!"

Kyle "Right Quick" Allen in Ecuador

Kyle, was money or transportation. He assured me, "*No hay problema*. I got it all figured out. First," he said, "We gotta get us some kers."

"What's a kers?" I asked, thinking it might be a secret stash of sucres, Ecuador's currency.

"You know, Kers, the beer," he said.

"You mean Coors?" I clarified. "I'm pretty sure we're not gonna find any here." We were stationed in the remote Andean village of Lloa, which clung precariously to the face of an active volcano, Wawa Pichincha. There were only two general stores in town and they both sold the exact same provisions. Fortunately for us, one of those "essentials" was Pilsener, the national *cerveza* of Ecuador. We bartered for a case and enquired about a ride to Nono.

The shopkeeper told us there were no buses, but, because of the festival, we could easily hitch a ride. After only fifteen minutes and two Pilseners by the side of the road, we jumped in the back of an old decrepit pickup truck crammed with enormous propane canisters. Standing in the bed for an hour and a half, I flinched every time we hit a pothole.

Nono was the size of Lloa, but because of the event it had swelled to abnormal proportions. Like an anthill floating in floodwaters, the pueblo was crawling with activity. There were stalls crammed with merchandise and vendors hocking everything from Panama hats to baked crickets. There were children playing football on a dirt field and a band playing Andean folk music in the street. The younger men, including us, did shots of *trago*, Ecuadorian moonshine to bolster our courage. The main event was a test of *machismo*.

In the central plaza, they had erected a makeshift bullring. It was made from felled eucalyptus trees bound together with henequen twine. From top to bottom and all the way around, the fence was covered with rubberneckers. Women cradling babies in alpaca blankets, old men wearing tattered fedoras, farmers, merchants, and priests all clung to the rails. They were there to see farm league bulls and boys vie for a shot at the majors. The animals that were deemed mean enough would be sent to fight in Quito, and the men who fought them here would be awarded applause, garlands, and more *trago*.

The first few bulls to enter the ring were just happy cows. They could have easily starred in a television ad for Chick-fil-A or the California Milk Advisory Board. The animals just strolled around the ring chewing their cud. Kyle and I, along with dozens of other young men danced around the arena with the placid creatures.

Then, a ruminant obviously cut from a different hide entered the ring. It had shifty eyes and an unpleasant demeanor. It was big and ugly and had no interest in making cheese or chewing cud. The locals immediately sensed danger and streamed from the arena as if someone had yelled, "Fire!"

Not having that sense, or any sense at all, Kyle and I remained in the ring. The bull immediately turned to face its unworthy foreign adversaries. Smoldering snot shot from its nostrils as it pounded the turf with its polished black hoofs. The crowd started chanting, "*Grin-gos! Grin-gos!*" I wasn't sure if they were cheering for us or the bull.

Being a pragmatist, I carefully weighed my options. I could run for the fence and try not to get trampled or gored in the back; I could throw myself in front of the animal, save Kyle, and be memorialized as *muy macho*; or, like those insane acrobats from Minoan Crete, I could catapult over the Minotaur and become a Nono legend. As the raging bull approached though, reason quickly surrendered to instinct. It was fight or flight, or, in my case (No, I'm not proud!) hide. I pivoted on the balls of my feet, forklifted Kyle behind his armpits and, drawing strength from enough adrenalin to legally win the Tour de France, I thrust him like a shield at the oncoming beast. Kyle screamed and the audience howled. The bull, as surprised as anyone, unexpectedly stopped in its tracks only inches from my "friend's" flailing body.

The bull looked at Kyle; Kyle looked at the bull; and I looked at the back of Kyle's head. With no other reasonable option, Right Quick grabbed the proverbial bull by the horns. The bull shook its head in disbelief. Like a damselfly under a windshield wiper, Kyle sailed back and forth. When he finally let go, the bull took a few steps back, lowered its head and prepared for its final, and most likely fatal charge.

At that exact moment, a man far more *macho* (and/or *borracho* or drunk) than us ran into the ring and smacked the bull on its leathery ass. Fortunately for us, the fee-ble-minded bovine was easily distracted. He spun around to face his latest adversary, allowing us to beat a hasty retreat beneath the fence. The crowd booed and then turned its attention to the new matador.

As Kyle yelled at me, the drunk man hurled insults and expletives at the bull. "¡*Que camarón*!" he slurred. "What a shrimp you are!" ¡*Que niño*!! ¡*Que @#$%&*?!!!" ¡

Using his poncho as a cape, he jeered and taunted the angry animal. "*Toro!*" yelled the crowd as the bull charged past the man.

As the raging bull turned and charged again, the man stumbled and fell. Trago was getting the better of him. "¡*Corre!*" yelled the crowd. "Run!"

The man tried to get up, but it was too late. The bull was already on top of him. It reared its head and stabbed at the man. The crowd screamed.

Two men dressed as clowns and carrying large, bright-ly colored barrels ran into the ring to distract the ani-mal. When the bull turned to confront them, Kyle and I reached under the fence, grabbed the man by his boots, and dragged his body from the ring, leaving a long trail of blood in the dirt. A deep gouge ran from the man's right kneecap all the way up to his chest. Paramedics put him on a gurney and rushed him off to a waiting ambulance.

The bull was corralled and carted off to Quito. He had earned the right to fight another day on a much bigger stage.

Meanwhile, Kyle and I stood silently on the side of the road trying to thumb a ride back to Lloa. We were done with diversions; we were ready for more training.

———

To this day, whenever I speak to Kyle, he always starts off right quick, "No, I still haven't forgiven you for Nono!"

"I know," I say. "I know."

¡El Gringo Va a Morir!

It was the last race I ever ran.

I had only been at my site for a few months when I decided to enter a 10K in Cuenca, Ecuador. In retrospect, it was a huge mistake. I hadn't trained since college; my New Orleans lungs were still ill-equipped to extract oxygen from the thin mountain air; and my flatlander muscles could hardly summit a curb much less clamber up steep cobblestone mountain roads. Nonetheless, I was, well, Peace Corps confident. Like so many new volunteers, I had set my sights on *saving the world*; so surely, a piddling Andean road race would be nothing more than an effortless (and triumphant) walk in the park.

It wasn't.

From the get-go, an endless stream of barrel-chested descendants of Atawalpa and Pizzaro blew by me as though I were plodding on a treadmill. Battling cramps, altitude sickness, and, more painful still, humiliation, I wearily soldiered on. When I finally approached the finish line, (I'd prefer not to divulge my time) there were only two other non-contenders left in the running, an old man wearing rubber boots and a little girl without shoes. In an all-out "sprint" for the final twenty meters, I just barely managed to pull ahead of the barefooted child. Unfor-

With sheep and kids in Ecuador, ca. 1990

tunately, the old man, obviously inspired by the raucous
cheering from his great-grandchildren, clipped me at the
already well-trodden tape.

With my deflated ego in tow, I endured the hour and
a half bus ride and the forty-five-minute walk back to my
site thinking, "Surely, this will be the worst experience of
my entire Peace Corps career?!"

It wasn't.

The next morning, I woke up in a sea of sweat. My
lungs, two waterlogged Nerf footballs, struggled to ab-
sorb even the smallest droplets of air. I had a fever of 105
and my body felt as though it had been run over by every
Ecuadorian who had passed me the day before. On top
of the shame from Saturday's drubbing and besides the
ever-present and occasionally brutal giardia, I now had

pneumonia, and without immediate medical attention, would most likely die.

Lucky for me it was Sunday, *el día de mercado*, and my landlord, a renowned curandero or shaman was in town and stopped by for a quick visit. "*El joven Leonardito**," he said, "You look *muy mal. Que pasó?*" Delirious, I couldn't manage even a syllable in Spanish, English, or Quechua. "*No hay problema*," he said, "I'll make you feel better *muy rapido*." He then beat me about the head with a severed sloth paw, spit *trago* or South American moonshine in my face, said a short prayer to Saint Joseph, and then gave me a rusted cup of lukewarm herbal tea (spiked with *trago* no less). "You'll be *mejor* in a couple of hours," he assured me as he shut the door and headed off to the market.

I wasn't.

When I finally came to the stark realization that the curandero's "cure" had failed, I dragged myself from the grass-filled futon, toweled off, and began the slow, serpentine stagger into town. Along the way, I passed, (or I should say, "they passed me") a number of *campesinos*. "¡*Que borracho Leonardito*!" they said and cheered. "How drunk you are. Good for you!"

"*No, estoy enfermo*," I slurred in protest.

"Right?" they countered sarcastically. "We'll have to discuss this over *cervezas* in town. *Vámonos!*"

When I stumbled into Jima, the principal of the elementary school, who knew I didn't drink, or at least not at that hour, immediately recognized the severity of my con-

---

* Most Ecuadorians had trouble pronouncing my first name, so I went by Leonardo in honor of my favorite Renaissance man. The "ito" had to do with my slight stature.

dition. She took me into her office and had me lie down on a long white plastic table. "Señor Dunbar," she announced, "I have good news and bad." Starting with the latter, she said, "The doctor did not come this week; but you are in luck, the curandero is here." Barely treading water, my heart sank.

"I'm pretty sure I'm gonna need modern medicine?" I suggested. "How about *El Veterinario*?"

"I believe he's in Zhamar vaccinating alpaca. I'll send one of my students to retrieve him *PRONTO*."

Shivering, sweating, and gasping for breath on the cold Formica, I vaguely made out an announcement over the church loudspeaker, "*Ven a ver al gringo morir*! Come see the Gringo die!**" Even in my delirium, I found it a bit disconcerting.

Much later than "pronto," the vet finally appeared. By then, I had become the town's most popular market-side attraction and the room was packed with pedestrian rubberneckers. The vet herded them away and started digging around in his saddlebag. He pulled out a huge thermometer obviously designed for a part of a large animal's anatomy I didn't possess. After causing me to grimace and tear up, he told me the first of two things I already knew: "You are very sick Señor Dunbar and if you do not receive treatment I am afraid you will die." He then took out a jug of penicillin and a syringe with a needle the size of a chopstick and told me the second: "This may hurt."

It did!

** In some parts of Latin America "gringo" is considered a derogatory term. This was not the case in Ecuador. (We were also known affectionately as "Misters.")

At the risk of sounding hyperbolic, my scream could be heard in all twelve towns of the *parroquia*. It's also worth pointing out that several English curse words are well understood in even the most far-flung parts of the non-English speaking world.

Soon after the *shot heard round the Equator*, my fever miraculously broke. The vet left and the crowd, a bit disappointed, dispersed. About a half an hour later though, my temperature began to rise again and the principal called for the priest.

Father Meyer, a large German with an insatiable appetite for roasted guinea pig and Scottish whiskey, burst into the room and bellowed, "Señor Dunbar, I am here to give you your Last Rites!"

Remembering the priest had the only car in town, I countered, "How about a ride to the hospital instead?"

Bouncing down the road to Cuenca in the back of Father Meyer's dusty Mercedes Benz SUV, I thought to myself, "If I survive, surely my *Cuerpo de Paseo* will improve?"

It did. A lot.

Fear and Loathing
on the Inca Trail

After all these years, I still have flashbacks. When I see a child blindly strike a *piñata* or when I smell a rotten egg, the memory, lodged deep in my scarred bowels explodes to the surface. Like Marlon Brando in *Apocalypse Now*, I recall, "The horror, the horror."

———

"*¡Levántate Leonardito! ¡Vamos!*" the *campesino* or farmer yelled from the base of the hill. "Get up little Leonardo! Let's go!"

Like grilled cheese, I was pressed between a lumpy straw mattress and a stack of cheap coarse blankets. I didn't want to *levántate*; I was warm and reasonably content. I pretended not to hear. Moments later though, the *campesino* pounded on my front door causing shards of adobe to cascade down on my head. "*Deme un ratito*," I pleaded. "Give me a second. I'll be ready *en seguida*."*

The weather in the high equatorial Andes is strangely unpredictable. The sun, so close to the earth you can almost touch it, burns like a glass blowing furnace. When it's out, your skin blisters and you have to squint like Clint

* In Ecuador nothing happens quickly or "*en seguida*." "*Ya mismo*," sometime between now and the next zombie apocalypse, is more the norm.

121

Above the tree line in Ecuador

Eastwood in a Spaghetti Western. Cover it with a cloud though, and you'll quickly need crampons and an ice axe. Latitude and elevation are always at odds. Because of this, dressing for a trek along the Inca Trail,** especially on a Peace Corps budget, was extremely challenging. I threw on lots and lots of layers; filled a backpack with reinforcements, including gear for rain, hail, and brimstone; stuffed my feet into cheap, Chinese-made rubber boots,*** the traditional footwear of Ecuador; and then, regrettably, left the shelter of my humble abode.

** This was not actually part of the famous Inca Trail. Apparently, even the ancients avoided this route.

*** Even though they make plenty of sense in South Louisiana where I'm from (see Cajun attire), I refuse to wear rubber boots to this day.

I had promised the *campesino* I would visit his farm. He raised sheep and alpaca but was looking to diversify his stock. He wanted to channel water from an irrigation ditch into an earthen pond and stock it with *trucha de arco iris*, rainbow trout. I had started a couple of fish projects downriver and owned a water quality test kit and a thermometer, which, in the Parroquia of Jima, made me an expert on aquaculture.

We walked along a narrow ridge just above the Rio Moya. The higher we climbed, the smaller and fewer the trees. Eventually, there would be nothing but dry grass or *paja*. Author's note: the lack of trees figures prominently in my PTSD haunted memories.

About thirty minutes into the two-and-a-half-hour hike, I released a rather inconspicuous burp. Unfortunately, it carried with it the unmistakable scent of sulfur, a telltale sign of giardiasis. Ordinarily, I would have simply popped a few Flagyl**** and soldiered on; but, in my haste, (see "ready *en seguida*") I hadn't packed the Roundup-like super drug. So, instead, I turned to my compañero and begged, "Amigo, is there any chance we could do this another day? *No me siento bien*. I don't feel well."

"Oh Leonardo," he implored, "we're so close. *Por favor, es muy importante*." I thought to myself, "We weren't exactly

**** Like Drano, Flagyl is fairly toxic. It's supposed to be taken sparingly in regimented doses. For over two years I popped them like Gummy Bears. I also didn't wear sunscreen, trekked up and down the Andes in cheap rubber boots, and drank way too much aguardiente. Like drinking water from an open irrigation ditch, I'm pretty sure these other youthful indiscretions are going to come back to haunt me as well.

close and it definitely wasn't all that important." He then pulled out a rusty flask containing his own home-distilled super drug, *aguardiente*. He handed me a shot and toasted, ironically, to health, "¡*Salud*!"

I winced down the kerosene-like concoction hoping it might at least momentarily appease the angry parasites in my gut, and continued along the winding path. It was at that time, between belches, that I had a jarring revelation, a "revelation" that should have been included in some Peace Corps pre-service manual. I noticed that the irrigation ditch, diverted from and channeled above the Rio Moya, flowed below acres and acres of pastureland used by *campesinos* to graze cattle, sheep, goats, and other livestock. It was this same irrigation ditch that supplied my humble abode with *agua potable* or drinking water. "Hmmmm," I thought, "that *agua* is probably not all that *potable* after all?"

And then, not unexpectedly, there was a second, larger and more pungent sulfuric belch. It was followed by a slow eruption of saliva, another telltale sign of impending doom. I called out to the farmer, "*Amigo, me siento muy, muy mal*. I feel awful. I have to return!"

Before he could offer me another well-intended shot of *firewater*, he actually recognized my dire situation. He saw the beads of sweat welling up on my exposed skin, skin that was now bone white and ice cold. He also heard the desperation in my cracking voice. He knew better than to push on. He said, "Leonardito, *no hay problema*. Perhaps we could do it another day?" He tipped his hat as though at a funeral, and walked ahead.

I spun around and took several shaky steps in the opposite direction. I wanted to get away; I wanted to hide.

I looked up and down for shelter. A Pot-O-Gold portal-et would have been ideal, though I would have happily settled for a tree—My kingdom for a tree! Unfortunately, there was nothing but paja, miles and miles of knee-high paja. At that point, like an exhausted gazelle in the Seren-geti surrounded by lions, hyenas, and vultures, I simply stopped and waited for nature to take its grisly course.

They say the male human body has six major orifices: eyes, ears, nose, mouth, anus, and urethra. All six of mine, along with thousands and thousands of pores, simultane-ously erupted.

Stuff, gallons of stuff my body obviously didn't want, sailed helter-skelter in all directions. I had control over nothing. My layers of cotton and wool absorbed as much as they could with the less viscous excess rolling down my flanks. Like clogged gutters in a toxic storm, my rubber boots, those damn rubber boots, filled to the brim and then overflowed. My backpack, worthless and forlorn, simply hung on for the ride. From afar, I must have looked like a clay pigeon struck by multiple shells. Up close, I looked and smelled like death.

I vaguely remember seeing the *campesino* glance over his shoulder, cringe, and then pick up his pace. I also not-ed that the cows and sheep on the hill coughed up extra cud in disgust.

Slogging my way back down the Rio Moya, filled with fear and loathing on the Inca Trail, I muttered, "The hor-ror, the horror."*****

***** Besides being hot, irritable, sliced up with a machete, and to-tally insane, Colonel Walter E. Kurtz in *Apocalypse Now* probably also suffered from dysentery.

¡Sigue no más!
Through the Quagmire of Despair

Author's Note: "*¡Sigue no más!*" in Spanish means, "Continue no more!" or, "Stop!" In Ecuador though, it had become a popular expression meaning, "Carry on," or, in my case, "Soldier on!"

———

When Mike Wooley stepped off the bus, he was carrying a vintage canvas Boy Scout backpack, an entire wheel of farmer's cheese, and a case of Pilsener, Ecuador's version of Milwaukee's Best. "*¡Listo!*" he exclaimed. "I'm ready!"

I had two bags of homemade granola, a box of iodine tablets, and a small tarp. I figured I was "listo" as well.

Wooley and I had planned to spend our Peace Corps "Spring Break" in the Amazon. We would climb over the Andes and drop down into the jungle. There, we would fish for piranha, learn the secrets of "*la selva*" from a wise shaman, and spot scarlet macaws, spectacled caiman, and red howler monkeys. It would be the adventure of a lifetime.

It was. But not in the way we had imagined.

That night we shared the Pilsner with friends from town. "*¡Dos días, pura bajada, y sequísimo!*" they said. The trip would take no more than two days, would be almost

My friend Mike Wooley in
Ecuador

entirely downhill, and,
even though it was the
rainy season, would be
bone dry. Upon hearing
this, Wooley began to
hum the theme song from
Gilligan's Island. It would
become a painful refrain.

The following morning, we asked a farmer for directions. He simply pointed at the cloud forest above town and said, "¡*Sigue no más!*"

As soon as Wooley, my dog Iko, and I set out on our adventure, the rain began to pour. For the next five days it rarely stopped.

The first six hours were straight up. (So much for, "*pura bajada!*") The air was thin and the trail was steep. Neither of us, excluding Iko, was in Sherpa shape. Every fifteen minutes or so we had to stop and gasp for breath.

We trudged over deep ruts carved by the hoofs of livestock, cows, pigs, and goats that had undoubtedly been as miserable as us! With every step, we slipped a half step back. Or, we got stuck. At one point, Wooley fell backward like a failed limboist. His boots were deep in one rut and his backpack was trapped in another. Like a tipped over tortoise, he flailed helplessly. When I finally stopped laughing, I pried him out with a eucalyptus limb.

Above the cloud forest, the path disappeared and the rain turned to sleet. Dressed for the Amazon and without a map or GPS, we wandered about shivering on the cold desolate high plateau.

That night, the three of us slept huddled beneath my tiny tarp, frozen bullets pelting our makeshift shelter.

The following morning, we finally found a pass through the mountains. On the other side, we took a narrow trail that zigzagged its way down a steep ravine, again, over unforgiving ruts. At the bottom, in a picturesque fog-cloaked valley, we entered the tiny town of San Miguel de Cuyes, or Saint Michael of the Guinea Pigs. It was an oasis in the desert, a temporary reprieve from the quagmire of despair. The locals put us up in an empty one-room schoolhouse. Apparently, the teacher hadn't shown up that year, so we had a dry place to stay. They gave us a bowl of "locro de papa" and, in honor of the

Mike Wooley and I in Ecuador, ca. 1990

town's patron saint, two roasted guinea pigs.

On the morning of the third day, in the rain, a farmer passed us at a gallop. He was carrying a huge sack of potatoes, two chickens, and a child. "How much farther to Gualaquiza?" we asked.

"*¡Dos días, pura bajada, y sequísimo!*" he said. "*¡Sigue no más!*"

As we descended into "la selva," or jungle, stunted shrubs were replaced by towering trees and trickling steams turned to raging rivers. With every step down, the temperature rose by a degree. The humidity was as thick as syrup and insects swarmed even thicker. We stripped down to our shorts and the rain steamed off our bodies.

On the fourth day, we plodded along in silence, using the leaves from elephant ear plants to shield us from the strafing rain. The granola and cheese were long gone by then, and the iodine tablets had dissolved in their box. We dreamed of dining on monkeys felled by poison darts, we drank untreated water from rivers and ruts, and we sang, "Just sit right back / And you'll hear a tale / A tale of a fateful trip, / That started from this tropic port, / Aboard this tiny ship…"

Teddy Roosevelt on *The River of Doubt* had had an easier journey.

On the morning of the fifth day, we staggered into Gualaquiza, a tiny outpost on the edge of the Amazon. "*¡Gracias a Dios!*" Wooley exclaimed. "Civilization at last!" According to Wooley, "civilization" was a place where you could get a hot shower and a shave. Gualaquiza just barely fit the bill.

Unlike Louis Zamperini, the WWII prison camp survivor, we were definitely not "unbroken." We were exhaust-

Walking into the town of San Miguel de los Cuyes

ed, famished, sick, and, it goes without saying, wet to the marrow. We were also short on sucres, the Ecuadorian currency. So, we decided to abandon our Amazonian adventure and take the red-eye back to the Andes.

After our shower and shave, we ate at the only restaurant in town. Its menu consisted of three items: breakfast, lunch and dinner. We each ordered two "dinners."

Knowing the bus ride would be a nightmare, Wooley and I proceeded to drink ourselves into a stupor. We bought a bottle of aguardiente, sanctioned Ecuadorian moonshine, and did shots with local jungle prospectors. Our plan was to pass out on the bus and wake up twelve hours later in the beautiful colonial town of Cuenca. Our brilliant plan though, had a fatal flaw: the size of our bladders.

About an hour into the trip, deep in the rainforest (and the rain), I stirred from my stupor. I had to pee.

Fortunately, the bus soon stopped. "It has to be a rest area," I thought.

(It wasn't. It was a military checkpoint. The Ecuadorian government was on the hunt for the notorious and elusive Colombian drug lord, Pablo Escobar.)

The isle was packed with livestock and supplies; there was no way I could possibly get off in time. So, I pushed Iko off my lap and climbed out the window. Still "*bien borracho*" or drunk, I tumbled to the ground like a sack of crawfish and landed on my back in deep mud. As I fell, I heard someone scream, "*¡Don Pablo!*"

When I looked up, I squinted through a blinding light and saw three machinegun barrels pointed at my face.

"*¿Pablo Escobar?*" a soldier barked.

"No," I said, "stupid gringo. "*¡Estoy chuchaqui y tengo que urinar!* I'm hungover, and I have to pee really bad!"

"Do you have an ID?" he asked.

"No," I said, "but I do have a friend and a dog on the bus who can vouch for me."

"What is the dog's name?" the soldier asked.

"Iko," I slurred.

"Doesn't Iko mean dog in Quichua?" he enquired.

"Yes," I said, "but it's spelled differently. I named her after a popular song in my hometown. It's just a coincidence."

The soldier, a bit perplexed, looked at the other men and then called out to his commander, "He's too skinny and white to be Don Pablo. And, he's got a dog named dog."

The soldiers laughed as the commander ordered me to get back on the bus.

Covered in mud and shame, I took my seat with "*All-*

cu," peed in an empty bottle of aguardiente, and went back to sleep.

About fifteen minutes later, there was a sobering rumble and the bus suddenly listed to one side. We had been hit by a mudslide. There was absolute pandemonium inside. Chickens, goats, and people all clambered for a way out. Once again, I was forced to climb through a window. We spent the next three hours excavating the partially buried bus.

Finally, the driver yelled, "*¡Sigue no más!*" and the bus lumbered forward.

At daybreak, we reached the crest of the Andes. It was, at last, "*pura bajada*." To save gas, the driver turned off the engine and tobogganed down the other side of the mountain. After several hairpin turns, my stomach lurched in protest. I immediately yelled for a "*funda*" or plastic bag, but it was already too late. I lunged over the woman seated next to me as a torrent erupted from my mouth. For a brief second I was relieved to have missed the woman and cleared the bus. But, alas, my relief was short-lived. The "torrent" was sucked back in through the next three open windows and sprayed the entire back of the bus. It was a dirty bomb and the collateral damage was extensive. So much for Peace Corps diplomacy!

At this point I was pretty sure I had hit the bottom of the quagmire of despair, a sad place indeed. But, I hadn't.

As soon as we reached the Pan American Highway, we slammed into a horse. There was a violent "Thud!" The bus bucked twice and then careened off the side of the road. Passengers shrieked, looked back in horror at the convulsing animal, and then, as if on cue, yelled, "¡*Sigue no más!*"

And, we did.

"¡*Sigue no más!*" I thought, "Yes, soldier on!"

Cotopaxi or Bust

*A Louisiana Flatlander's
Misadventures in the High Andes*

In the Armpit of the Pacific*

"The ceviche smells fishy," I said.

"Of course, it smells fishy Sherlock," said Mike. "It's &%$#ing FISH!"

"I know," I said, "but it just doesn't *seem* right."

"Dude, we're on the &%$#ing beach," he said. "It's gotta be fresh!" Mike took a small bite, rolled the lime-*cooked* flesh over his tongue, winced and spit it out on the sand. "OK, maybe you're right."

We were in the seaside town of Esmeraldas on the Pacific coast of Ecuador. According to *Lonely Planet*, "Esmeraldas is ugly, dangerous, and dirty, and there's really no reason to stay there." Yet, there we were.

Mike and I were on our Christmas Break from Peace Corps. We were looking to experience "the real" Ecuador, warts and all. Esmeraldas seemed as good a place as any.

---

* Esmeraldas is actually an interesting town. Settled by escaped slaves in the sixteenth century, it was one of the largest maroon communities in Spanish South America. Its residents developed a distinctive style of music called currulao and a popular coconut seafood stew called encocado. The city has also produced some of Ecuador's finest football (soccer) players.

Later that night, I heard a grumbling from the top bunk. I figured either Mike had gotten "lucky" at a *chongo*, or he had had one too many *tragos*. Then, I heard a visceral bellow and the bed suddenly listed to one side. I looked up and caught Mike's silhouette sailing through the air like a flying squirrel that had misjudged the distance between two tree limbs. Midway to the floor, Mike violently exploded, spraying shrapnel in all directions, including mine. When he hit the dirt floor of our *palapa*, he was almost completely devoid of liquid. Lying in a shallow pool of his own plasma, he murmured, "Yeah, the ceviche was definitely bad!"

Mike spent the rest of the evening in a public latrine down the beach.

The next morning, two friends of ours arrived by bus from Santo Domingo. Paul and Steve were looking forward to a few days of sun, sand, and *cerveza*. Unlike us, they envisioned Spring Break in Fort Lauderdale, Cancun, or Montego Bay. After a quick survey of the gritty oil and banana port town though, their "Girls Gone Wild" bubble burst. "This place is the f%&ing armpit of the Pacific," said Steve. "There's no way I'm spending my vacation here!"

"Let's climb Cotopaxi instead," suggested Paul. Paul was from Colorado and was an avid mountaineer. His fourth** Peace Corps goal was to climb every major peak in the country.

** Officially, there are only three Peace Corps goals: 1) to help the people of interested countries in meeting their need for trained men and women, 2) to help promote a better understanding of Americans on the part of the peoples served, and 3) to help promote a better understanding of other peoples on the part of Americans. If there were a fourth goal, it would be for volunteers to survive (and learn from) boneheaded decisions.

"I'm in," said Steve.

"Sounds like an adventure," I said. "*¿Por qué no?* Why not?" Note: "In retrospect, "adventure" was a gross understatement and the answer(s) to my rhetorical question was patently obvious.

Mike, still a bit green from the ceviche, shrugged and said, "No, not me. I'd rather recover from food poisoning here; the air is warm and the beer is cold. I'm staying in 'the f%&ing armpit!'"

The Ascent into Madness

The next morning, the three of us jumped on a bus to Quito and climbed more than nine thousand feet up into the high Andes. In Ecuador's capital, we borrowed sweaters, jackets, and sleeping bags from volunteers in the city, and we rented climbing equipment: gaiters, crampons, carabiners, ice axes, and other gear I had only seen in movies and magazines. We then hired a driver to take us to the Jose F. Rivas refuge on the northern flanks of Volcán Cotopaxi, the tallest active volcano in the world.

On the ride up, Paul asked, "Have you ever been mountaineering?"

"Are you kidding?" I said. "I'm from Louisiana. Our highest peak is Mount Driskill, which, technically, isn't even a mountain. The levees and Monkey Hill are about as high as you get in New Orleans."

Two miles below the refuge, it started to rain. The dirt road quickly turned to mud and the driver abruptly stopped. "*No puedo seguir,*" he said. "I can't continue. You'll have to walk from here." We grabbed our heavy packs and began slogging our way up the mountain.

A half an hour later, Steve began to cough and wheeze. He could hardly breathe. "My head feels like it's in a vice," he complained, as blood trickled from his nose. Steve was suffering from a severe case of altitude sickness. The climb from sea level to fifteen thousand feet in one day had obviously been too much.

Paul and I took turns carrying Steve's pack. We arrived at the refuge just before dusk.

Our original plan was to spend at least one full day at the refuge acclimating to the high altitude. Now, we figured we'd have to take Steve back to Quito as soon as possible.

Steve, in addition to feeling bad, felt guilty. "Why don't you guys try to summit tonight?" he suggested. "You'd be back by 8:00. We could return to the city then. Who knows, I might even recover."

"Is it safe to climb at night?" I asked.

"You have to climb at night," said Paul. "Cotopaxi is almost on the equator. The intense heat from the sun during the day melts the snow and makes it too dangerous to climb. You try to summit by daybreak, enjoy the view at the top, and then hustle back down before the snow turns to sludge. I'm up for it if you are?"

Again, I foolishly replied, "*¿Por qué no?*"

Though almost twenty thousand feet above sea level, Cotopaxi is actually not a difficult climb. In 1802, the famous explorer, Alexander von Humboldt almost made it to the top without the benefit of fancy gear like carabiners or Patagonia goose down. "For an experienced climber under good conditions," said Paul, "it's practically a walk in the park." Unfortunately for me, neither of those was the case.

That night, we hung out with other climbers. We drank shots of warm canelazo, an Ecuadorian version of a hot toddy made with *aguardiente* or burning water, and we ate *locro de papas*, a traditional Andean soup from a communal pot.

In a sleeping bag obviously rated for milder temperatures, I spent the next four hours shivering—and awake.

At midnight, a group of about thirty climbers (and me) left the refuge. When we reached the edge of the glacier, we stopped to put on our crampons, tie in with other "mountaineers," and discuss the route. Paul used the opportunity to show me a few techniques, including the all-important self-arrest. "You probably won't need this on Cotopaxi," he assured me, "but, it could save your life some day."

I used the opportunity to contemplate the meaning of the word "probably" and the idea that people actually die while climbing mountains.

As soon as we got up on the ice, the winds picked up and snow began to fall. Soon, we were in an all-out blizzard. Visibility dropped to zero, and half the climbers wisely turned around. Paul and I stubbornly soldiered on.

Inching my way up in the darkness, my lungs began to seize up. I couldn't find the air. After every step, I had to stop and gasp for breath. I was like a fish in a stagnant pool desperately gulping at the surface.

Progress was painfully slow. I could sense my teammate's growing frustration. Like a massive barnacle on the bottom of a racing shell, I was holding them back. At this pace, we'd summit by Easter.

As we came upon a small cave on the side of the mountain, I said, "Y'all go on without me. I'll stay here and y'all can pick me up on the way down."

"You sure?" asked Paul, a bit guilty but also relieved.

"*Por supuesto*, of course," I lied.

Like the parents of *Pierre* in that cautionary tale by Maurice Sendak, "they left me there."

I crawled inside the cave, curled up in the fetal position and nursed (unsuccessfully) on thin air.

In my snowbound mausoleum, I thought about George Mallory on Everest, Sir Ernest Shackleton's ill-fated expedition to the South Pole on the *Endurance*, the Uruguayan rugby team that crashed in the Andes and ate each other to stay alive, the protagonist in that famous short story by Jack London, and *Jeremiah Johnson*, who catches on fire sleeping on hot coals. I tried to think of other things, more pleasant things, but I couldn't. My brain cells, deprived of oxygen, were in their own state of "self-arrest!"

My grim hallucinations soon morphed into a full-blown panic attack. I had no one to eat, no bed of coals to sleep on, no Sherpa to retrieve my body, nor dog to grieve my death. I was gonna die alone in a cave on the side of the world's tallest active volcano!

So, I picked myself up and resumed the ascent—into madness.

A few hundred yards below the volcano's crater, I ran into my team on its way down. They berated me for leaving the cave and climbing without a rope. But, I could tell they were also reasonably impressed. "He made it this far," said one of the climbers. "He deserves to summit."

"It's getting late," cautioned Paul, "but I agree. Let's give him a shot."

It was well after 8:00 o'clock when I finally reached the summit. They say on a clear day atop Cotopaxi, you can see both the Caribbean Sea and the Pacific Ocean. In the blinding sleet, I could hardly see my own frozen feet. Like Chevy Chase at the Grand Canyon in National Lampoon's *Vacation*, I looked over the edge, bobbed my head up and down and said, "OK, let's go."

Hanging from a Frayed Rope

In the confusion of the blizzard, we somehow missed the trailhead and came down off the wrong side of the mountain.

An hour later, we finally realized our mistake. We had two options: we could either climb back up or skirt around. The former would be longer and harder, while the latter would be technically more demanding but possibly quicker. Considering the clouds had passed and the equatorial sun was now cooking us like an Easy-Bake Oven, we opted for curtain number two.

After more than ten hours on the mountain, I could finally breathe. Now, I was just cold, tired, and hungry.

"Make sure you keep your crampons clean," warned Paul, whacking the bottom of his boots with the blunt end of his axe. "The snow is starting to melt!"

A few minutes later, having forgotten to clear my crampons, I took my first fall. I slipped on my ass and started tumbling down the side of the mountain. Remembering Paul's earlier tutorial, I rolled onto my side and plowed my ice axe into the snow. When I came to a stop, my teammates applauded. Note: After my fourth fall, they stopped

Climbing on Cotopaxi, ca. 1990

clapping and just stared at me with contempt.

At some point along the way, we came across a massive crevasse. "We'll have to build a snow bridge," exclaimed Paul! Paul was excited because he had never done the maneuver; I was terrified because Paul had never done the maneuver.

As I crawled across the bottomless, icy canyon on a makeshift ladder, I looked down and discovered for the first time that I am acrophobic. The timing of course could not have been worse. My climbing companions, *por supuesto*, found it both predictable and amusing!

It took a while, but we crossed the crevasse and continued our descent.

Finally, after more than sixteen hours of climbing, we reached the edge of the glacier. Paul gave a stern warning, obviously directed at me, "Be careful, the ice is slick!"

Before the last syllable left his now chapped lips, my feet kicked up into the air and I fell flat on my chest. Like an Olympic skeleton racer, I flew down the side of the mountain. As I had done several times before, I rolled onto my side and leaned into my axe, causing a rooster tail of ice to arc up into the air behind me. But, I didn't stop. Instead, I sailed off into the abyss.

The force and weight of my free-falling body yanked two other climbers down after me. Only Paul and one other remained. For a brief moment, they actually considered cutting us loose. Instead, they jammed their ice axes into the rock, dug in with their crampons and braced for impact.

Unlike a bungee cord, the rope had almost no elasticity. The jolt was, well, jarring. It caused me to drop my axe, compressed several vertebrae, and chipped my front tooth. I came to an abrupt stop and careened back into the hard rock face of Cotopaxi, ripping off a gaiter, tearing my borrowed down jacket, and smashing my nose. But, I was alive!

Hanging by a frayed rope like a corpse from the gallows, I thought to myself, "I'd rather be eating spoiled ceviche in the Armpit of the Pacific," and "Thank God for frayed rope!"

Epilogue

It took us another hour and a half to get back on and off the glacier. By the time we finally made it back to the refuge, the sun was setting off the coast of Esmeraldas. We had been climbing for more than eighteen hours straight! Steve had already gone back to the city and had checked himself into the Peace Corps infirmary. Paul and I hitched a ride in the cab of a supply truck back to Quito. I slept at a hostel for two days before heading back to my site.

Paul told me he had never been on a climb where there had been so many falls. It was a dubious distinction and cold comfort,*** especially considering it cost me more than a month's per diem to replace the equipment I had destroyed.

When I finished my stint in *Cuerpo de Paz*, I moved back to the flatlands of Louisiana. Apart from summiting an occasional levee, I haven't climbed since!

*** Speaking of cold comfort, whenever I play that team-building game where you have to list two truths and a lie, I always include "falling off the world's tallest active volcano."

Luv Ledders
Leading to a Close Encounter
of a Salacious Kind

For a while I was the only male faculty member at an all-girls school. It was, well, a bit surreal. Thanks to my Y chromosome, I got way more attention than I deserved. I was seen as either a rock star, a duck-billed platypus, or a clump of cold, overcooked broccoli.

In some ways, my novelty was an asset. Teaching high school history is like selling sand in the Sahara; I needed all the help I could get. So, I leveraged my testosterone like Napoleon's reserves at Austerlitz, and won a handful of hard fought, lesson planned battles.

For obvious reasons, my gender was also a distraction and a liability. Some students were more interested in my skinny ties and Adam's apple than the Platt Amendment or the New Deal. At times, I felt like Indiana Jones in the college classroom scene from *Raiders of the Lost Ark*. I would have been more comfortable dodging Mayan boulders or Egyptian snakes.

Then, about halfway through the first semester of my first year teaching, my worst fear came true. I went home and found a letter in my mailbox. The envelope was pink and scented. Inside, the handwriting was almost illegible. It was packed with misspelled words, grammatical errors, little hearts, and cute squiggles. When I read it, my stomach wrenched. It was a love letter—obviously from a student.

The next day, I ran straight to the principal's office and showed her the letter. (Note: I considered taking it to the English Department as well.) She told me not to worry. "Crushes like this are fairly common," she said. "They're usually innocent and short lived. If you get another letter, just let me know."

Later that day during my planning period, a student walked into my classroom and shut the door behind her. It creaked like a casket closing. She had questions about a project I had assigned. As she spoke, all I could hear were the lyrics to the song, "Don't Stand So Close to Me" by The Police: "Young teacher, the subject / Of schoolgirl fantasy / She wants him so badly / Knows what she wants to be…"

A week later, another letter arrived. It was even more salacious than the first. Again, I took it to the principal's office. On my way there, I heard, "Loose talk in the class-room / To hurt they try and try / Strong words in the staffroom / The accusations fly…"

The principal sent me to the guidance counselor, who gave me a bevy of strategies to avoid "awkward situa-tions." She told me to never meet with a student alone and to always keep my door open. She also suggested that I do a little CSI work while grading papers. "This student is a really bad writer," she said. "Put on your William Strunk hat and connect the dangling modifiers."

The third letter (with significant editing) could have been published in Penthouse Magazine. It was more graphic than a Frank Miller novel; it was fifty shades of plaid. It caused me "to shake and cough, just like the old man in that book by Nabokov."

I bought a newspaper that day and started looking through the help-wanted ads.

At the time, I lived in a tiny studio apartment on Magazine Street in Uptown New Orleans. I slept on a futon in a second floor loft. My bookshelf-like bedroom faced a huge window that overlooked the street. On the other side, there was a house with a window facing mine. One night while I was lying in bed, a woman drew the curtains on the other side and launched into a striptease. When she finished, she pressed her naked body against the window. Cars passing by below honked in either shock or appreciation.

She performed again the following evening. And then again and again.

"WTF!?" I thought. "Now, in addition to a student stalker, I have a crazy neighbor auditioning in her window for a Bourbon Street gig! Maybe I should move to a small town in the Midwest? I could teach at an all-boys school—a military academy perhaps?"

The following Friday, I stayed out late playing pool at a local pub. I tried to drown my anxiety in Dixie Beer.

A few minutes after I got home, my doorbell rang. It was the woman from the window. She was standing on my stoop wearing nothing but a bathrobe. When I opened the door, she dropped the robe to the ground. "I know you want me," she said.

"No, I really don't," I replied.

"Didn't my letters make you hot?" she asked.

"You wrote those letters?!" I gasped with relief. "No, they actually made me ill. And, they almost cost me my career!"

"Give me one good reason you don't want this?" she said, gesturing to her pale naked body.

"I can give you five," I said. "1) You're married (to a policeman no less), 2) you have a child, 3) I have a girlfriend, 4) I'm not that attracted to you, and 5) your writing is atrocious!"

The next day I bought a sheet and duct taped it to the window.

A New Orleans Horror Story

It was, without a doubt, the worst experience of my life. Ever!

One time I actually sat down and ranked my bottom ten. They included a hellacious bout with Montezuma's revenge, a bullet ant sting to my left big toe, and falling off the world's highest active volcano. They all somehow pale in comparison. Yes, this one was definitely the worst.

———

I lived in a studio apartment on Magazine Street in New Orleans. It had one large room, a kitchenette, and a bathroom the size of an armoire. There was a spiral staircase that led to a loft just wide enough to squeeze in a single mattress on an old iron frame from the old Ursuline Convent. There was a window next to the bed that faced the adjacent building and a much needed but extremely annoying security light.

I had just returned from a two-and-a-half-year stint in the Peace Corps and was suffering from an acute case of reentry shock. I had stubbornly convinced myself that I would someday soon return to my Luddite life in Ecuador, so I refused to succumb to the lure of modern amenities. I didn't want to get soft. As a result, I didn't use AC or heat, and I didn't have a phone or TV. (And, as a result, I wasn't in a relationship.)* My NOLA apartment was basically a glorified tent.

It was a typical balmy August night in the Crescent City. The temperature outside was an almost tolerable 85 degrees. In my Dutch oven tent though, it was a good 10 degrees higher. And, in my upstairs rotisserie, it had to be pushing a hundred. I lay in bed wearing nothing but sweat. I was trying to read a book, *Dante's Inferno* I believe, but it kept slipping from my perspiration-soaked hands. There was a small electric fan pointed at my head. Its narrow shaft of wind created a tiny desert on my face, a desert surrounded by the vast oasis of my greenhouse apartment. I had begun to yawn, so I dropped the book, pretended to turn out the light from the window, and closed my eyes.

At that exact moment, a palmetto bug** the size of a small Andean condor, flittering on the summer night thermals radiating off the hot asphalt below and gunning for the security light in the alley, flew in through my open bedroom window. It immediately got caught in the fan's crossfire wind and was hurled toward the black hole of my final yawn.

I distinctly remember the sound. It was as if a large plastic ball had been sucked down a storm drain in a flash

---

* When I met my future wife, she of course had (and used) air-conditioning. It was only a matter of summer nights before I became addicted to her and her *sacred air*!

** *Periplaneta americana*, the American cockroach is not a palmetto bug, but, it sure sounds better to have eaten the latter.

flood. It made a sudden and violent "Thwoop!"

I tried to scream, but my vocal chords were clogged. Like a cat desperately trying to cough up an enormous hairball, I gasped and choked. But the more I did, the deeper it went. The creature had little grappling hooks on its spindly legs. Obviously designed for scampering up walls and across ceilings, they were now clawing at the tender lining of my mouth and throat.

As I pushed out, the insect dug in.

Gasping for breath, and without a witness to perform the Heimlich maneuver, I came to the painful realization that extraction was not an option. There was only one direction to go.*** I clinched my eyes shut, grabbed the headboard of the nuns' bed and swallowed—and swallowed...

In retrospect, I actually feel bad for the roach. He was probably just enjoying a lovely summer night in the city, sailing about minding his own business. I'm sure he had big plans: dining on picnic leftovers at The Fly, hanging with the Formosan krewe beneath some cool street lamp, or perhaps catching a set by the Cucarachas on Frenchmen Street? Instead, he got sucked into a New Orleans horror story written by Franz Kafka and directed by David Cronenberg. It was a frightening (and fatal) experience for him as well.

*** It's important to point out that this happened long before my friend, Zack Lemann from the Audubon Insectarium cooked bugs for Jay Leno on The Tonight Show and made eating insects somewhat fashionable.

Lesson Plans Gone Awry

Author's Note: Over the years, I've done all kinds of crazy stunts to get kids (and adults) fired up about learning. From dressing up as a superhero named Geography Man, to conducting archeological digs in garbage dumps, they were all well-intended, though occasionally ill-conceived. While most of my lesson and project plans worked out, a few did crash and burn. I figured I could always justify the failures, as long as there was a connection, albeit flimsy, to the curriculum. I usually could—but not always.

Making Sausage

I once took a group of seventh-grade girls on a trek across Louisiana. We were only gone for four days and three nights, but it took years off my life!

One of the many stops along the way was Savoie's Cajun Products in Opelousas. The company specialized in making smoked sausage, andouille, and boudin.

I chose Savoie's because the owner was a woman. I thought she would be a good role model for my kids. It was also a great example of a successful, homegrown business. And besides, what's more Louisiana than spicy meat products?

In my classroom, ca. 1995

Ms. Savoie was pumped up like a Ball Park Frank. "We don't get many school groups," she admitted. "Matter of fact, y'all might just be the first!"

As we entered the factory, I quickly discovered why.

The building looked like the prop room from a Wes Craven movie set. There were freezers and smoke rooms filled with hanging, flayed animal cadavers, huge contraptions for grinding up meat and bone, and massive tubs filled with pulverized flesh. The floor was tinted red from blood and the air smelled like sanitized death.

I met a woman who had spent her entire life, eight hours a day, five days a week, inspecting miles and miles of sheep intestines for tears and other defects; and there was a man carefully patrolling the floor, scooping up and "recycling" spilt viscera. The owner proudly pointed out, "We don't waste anything here. It's a very efficient operation."

The operation was also efficient at taking out kids. Within minutes, my squeamish middle schoolers began to drop like bald cypress needles in winter. High-pitched shrieks were accompanied by a chorus of, "Like, Oh - My - God!"

Several girls bolted for the bathroom; a few didn't make it. The tour was like an accelerated and rather gross version of the reality TV show, *Survivor*. I extinguished one Cajun tiki torch after another.

At the end of the tour, the few students who remained were offered a smorgasbord of samples. Needless to say, there weren't many takers.

When I got back to school, the principal and I were bombarded by calls from irate parents. They complained that their kids had been permanently traumatized by the fieldtrip. "My daughter converted to vegetarianism!" cried one parent.

"What could kids possibly learn by visiting a sausage factory?!" barked another.

"Well," I replied, "the USDA does recommend that our kids eat more vegetables. And, we definitely learned that the adage about laws and sausage is true: you really don't want to see either one being made!"

"You Could Have Put an Eye Out!"

I once did a unit on ancient weapons. My class and I discussed the Claw of Archimedes, Greek Fire and the Trojan Horse, boomerangs, bows, and bolas. We made bamboo spears with Play-Doh points and hurled them across the yard using a makeshift atlatl; and, armed with Styrofoam swords and cardboard shields, we reenacted famous battles like Kadesh, Thermopylae, and Salamis.

I also brought in an authentic blowgun from the Amazon. I had picked it up in Ecuador where I had served as a Peace Corps volunteer years before. I had long since lost the darts though, so I had to improvise by using pushpins and laundry lint. I didn't have any poison dart frogs either, so I ceremoniously dipped the points in Elmer's glue.

For my demonstration, I put a dartboard on the door and huddled with my class on the other side of the room. As I prepared to fire, the kids, of course, yelled a line from Gary Larson's *The Far Side*: "Blow Mr. Dunbar, don't suck!"

I took in a deep breath, put the gun in my mouth, and exhaled as hard as I could. As the projectile exited

With my students after a
theatre performance

the long barrel, the door
to my room suddenly
cracked open, and my
principal's head popped
in. The kids screamed as
the dart grazed her nose,
ricocheted off the door,
and stuck in the jacket la-
pel of another adult.

Apparently, my prin-
cipal was giving a tour of
the school to prospective parents and board members. She
wanted to show off my room. It was covered from floor to
ceiling with maps and globes, it had classroom pets and
plants, and there was a sandbox for staging archeological
digs. It was pretty cool, I have to admit.

As the audience for my blowgun demonstration stood
silently with gaping mouths, my principal said in a stern,
though surprisingly calm voice, "Mr. Dunbar, sorry for
the interruption. Could you please see me in my office
after school?"

In her office, I pleaded my case, citing World History
standards, research in support of experiential learning,
the concept of "appropriate technology," and the classic
book by Jared Diamond, *Guns, Germs, and Steel*.

"I don't particularly care Mr. Dunbar," she said. "You
could have put an eye out!"

The Pearl River Tea Party

I took a group of eighth-grade girls on a fieldtrip to the Honey Island Swamp. A friend of mine, Mr. Denny, had built two large voyageur canoes. Each one could carry as many as fifteen people. We loaded up the boats and headed into the swamp.

On the way back, we had to paddle upstream. The current in the Pearl River was strong; and Mr. Denny and I had to do the bulk of the work, since most of the girls were not accustomed to non-motorized vehicles. It was hot and I was thirsty. I yelled to Mr. Denny, "Ya got anything to drink?"

"Sweet tea," he replied.

"Could I have a swig?" I called back.

"Sure," he said. Mr. Denny reached into a waterproof duffle bag, pulled out a large plastic jug, and hurled it like a shotput in my direction. With my paddle in one hand, I caught the jug with the other. I could tell my students were impressed.

I gulped down some lukewarm tea, and prepared to toss the container back. It seemed like a simple task, throwing a plastic jug a few yards. But, in reality, it wasn't. It was like an SAT question with lots of variables. I had to factor in things like current speed and wind velocity, the sporadic movement of kids and paddles, and the constraints of throwing something from a seated position.

As it turns out, I missed the question and overshot my target. The heavy jug sailed over the canoe, clipping a girl on the shoulder, and landed in the water like an errant cannonball. The startled passengers all jostled in

Taking my kids into the Honey Island Swamp, ca. 1995

their seats, causing one poor student to tumble awkward-
ly overboard.

In that brief moment between the first and second
splash, I saw my entire career in education, albeit brief,
flash before my eyes.

After the short, nostalgic reel, I quickly turned the boat
around, raced after the flailing child, and fished her out
of the river. "It's a good thing I required them to wear life
jackets," I thought.

On the ride back to school, the girls excitedly jabbered
on about the incident, while I desperately cobbled together my feeble "curriculum" defense. It included references
to the Boston Tea Party and Washington crossing the Del-
aware, research in support of tough, character building

exercises, and, of course, the pedagogy of learning by getting your feet—and other body parts—wet.

As I made my way down the hallway toward the principal's office, I could have sworn I heard an announcement over the intercom: "Dead man walking!"

I felt like Sir Thomas More on his way to meet Henry VIII for the last time, only I was no *Man for All Seasons*! I was just a humble middle school history teacher (and an amateur swamp tour guide) whose lesson plans had gone terribly awry.

Ending with a Splash
And Surviving an
Elementary School Sharknado

When we were kids, our parents used to take us to Destin, Florida, for summer vacation. Unlike the Louisiana Coast, the sand was white, the water was blue, and the horizon was completely free of oilrigs. It was (and still is) pretty amazing. We spent the entire day splashing in the surf. When our parents finally dragged us out of the water for dinner, we were shriveled up like little naked mole rats.

That all changed the year we saw *Jaws*. After seeing the film, to our parent's dismay, we refused to step foot in the water—for years!

I can only imagine that my shark "presentation" many years later had a similar effect.

———

I used to bring animals to schools. I would showcase a different group each month. There were snakes, turtles, raptors, rodents, and spiders. I called it, "Mr. Dunbar's Featured Creature."

The kids loved it. According to them, "It was like the best show and tell EVER!"

For my final presentation of the year, I brought in sharks. As I told the teachers, "I want to end with a splash!"

True to my word, I did.

Because sharks need salt water, lots of salt water, I couldn't exactly bring in live specimens. Instead, I had eight large jars of embryos and pups, all swimming in formaldehyde. I loaded the jars, along with teeth, mermaid purses, skins, pictures, and models onto a library cart and wheeled it from one class to the next. I wore a shark hat, plastic jaws, and blue fin mitts.

My last presentation of the day was for a combined class of kindergarteners and first graders. Like chum scattered around a charter boat, they had gathered together on the carpeted floor of the school library. They were pumped up like frightened puffer fish.

I was late for the show, so I was pushing the cart a bit faster than the recommended speed in the Teacher Handbook.

As I entered the room, the front casters slammed into the reducer molding, causing the cart to suddenly stop and buck. It tipped over and catapulted its contents into the audience.

The jars exploded like massive Molotov cocktails, spraying the kids with formaldehyde and embryos. The screams were deafening. There were torrents of tears. It was like a scene from *Sharknado*, or, an entire month of *Shark Week* condensed into a single, terrifying moment.

Pandemonium spread like lice, and the once happy elementary school was forced into lockdown.

The kids were inconsolable. Parents and grandparents were called in to do triage, as counselors and social workers frantically consulted the state's Crisis Management Manual.

Like Pee-wee Herman or O.J. Simpson, my fame quickly turned into infamy. Kids and teachers alike glared at me with utter disdain.

A huge asteroid had once again crashed into the Gulf of Mexico, and now all my well-intended "featured creatures" were heading for extinction.

Sitting with the principal at a bar later that night, I joked, "I think I needed a bigger cart!"

He got the reference, but didn't (couldn't) laugh.

When I visited the school the following year, I could still sense the terror in the children's eyes. Walking down the hallway, I could also vaguely make out the score from *Jaws*, pulsing like a tell-tale heart beneath the floor.

The Bellman's Cart Derby

Guy Harrington was enormous. A former heavyweight high school wrestler from Nebraska, he tipped the scales at just under three hundred pounds. I affectionately referred to him as, "The Big Guy."

I had wrestled in college at 133 and hadn't grown much since. Not surprisingly, he called me, "The Little Guy."

We worked for an educational company that specialized in project-based teaching and learning. We were setting up for a conference at a hotel in Downtown Atlanta. The hotel was located at the top of a tall, steep hill. We were using bellman's carts to haul in books, handouts, brochures, and projectors.

As we were wrapping up, I turned to Guy and said, "Dude, I've got a project idea!"

"What's that?" he asked.

"Let's ride one of these luggage racks down the hill. It would be like soapbox derby!"

"How's that a project?" asked Guy.

"We could estimate the time to the bottom based on slope, distance, and mass. We could talk to teachers about other variables like wheel diameter, friction, wind velocity, and barometric pressure."

"And stupidity!" added Guy. "You obviously weren't a

physics major!"

"No," I admitted, "but it would be a real-world project. We could talk about it in our session tomorrow."

"People don't ride luggage racks in the real world!"
said Guy.

"It would be fun though," I replied with a devious grin.

"True," said Guy. "OK, but just one run…"

The Big Guy squeezed into the front of our makeshift
toboggan. I pushed off and hopped on the back. Within
seconds, we were barreling down the hill.

"We've got too much inertia," I cried!

"You don't know what inertia means, do you?" replied Guy.

"No," I said, "but we *are* out of control!"

The wobbly little casters on the cart, obviously not designed for high-speed racing, shrieked in protest, and the
rickety aluminum frame bucked like a tempestuous bull.

I tried to steer (pun intended), but gravity would have
none of it (Damn you, Sir Isaac Newton!), and the rubber soles of my Chuck Taylors were useless as brakes.
We were on a collision course with a busy intersection
at the bottom of the hill. We would surely be squashed
like that frog in the popular video game from the 1980s.
I had to act fast!

With all my might (and 133 pounds), I thrust myself
against the back-right post. The cart abruptly twisted on its
axis and I was tossed from my coxswain's perch. Without
my weight, the luggage rack took a nosedive and plowed
into the pavement. The Big Guy was catapulted into the air
like a massive projectile from a trebuchet. As he tumbled
across the sky, pedestrians screamed and frantically dialed

911, small children pointed up and peered in wonder, and squirrels and pigeons scurried away for cover. I know it was inappropriate, but, lying on the street, I couldn't help but crack a smile at the absurdity of the scene.

Guy landed with a tremendous "Thud!" and skipped across the asphalt like an errant cannonball on the deck of a sailing ship from the Napoleonic Wars. He finally stopped at the curb, just inches before the intersection.

All the skin from his arms and legs had been flayed off. He looked like the carcass of a salmon that had been mauled by a bear and then picked over by ravenous eagles and ants. It was not a pretty picture. But, he was alive!

I ran up to the mountainous, bloody mass and cried, "Are you OK?!"

"What the &%$! do you think ya little shit?!" grumbled Guy. "You tried to kill me!"

"No," I retorted. "I saved your life! It was a John F&%$ing Kennedy Profile in Courage!"

"Courage my ass," said Guy. "You bailed! If I could move, I'd pummel ya right here!"

I kept my distance.

To this day, Guy and I still debate the legitimacy of my heroism.

Author's Note: My "real-world" project presentation, with its mangled bellman's cart and ex-friend in tow, was a huge success!

The Coup de Grâce for the Workshop that Didn't Work

In retrospect, I probably should have gone the day before and stayed the night. Instead, I got up early and drove. Like the famous shopping scene from *Pretty Woman*, it was a "BIG mistake!"

I was doing a presentation for a school in Franklin, Louisiana. I was anticipating a tough crowd. The school was not doing well academically, and, as a result, my workshop was a command performance from the DOE. To make matters worse, it was being held on a Saturday, the same day as the popular Crawfish Festival in the near-by town of Breaux Bridge.

Leaving New Orleans at four in the morning, I had plenty of time to spare. Unfortunately, though, there was a thick fog covering the Atchafalaya like a roux, and traffic on I-10 was backed up from Beaumont to Baton Rouge. At the little town of Sorrento, I took a detour. I turned south toward Morgan City and crossed the Mississippi on the Sunshine Bridge.

I figured it might be a shortcut.

It wasn't.

My trek across the swamp took longer than it did for John Hanning Speke to discover the source of the Nile. And, my journey was probably just as eerie as his. Among the misty cypress trees draped in Spanish moss, I couldn't help but think of the 1981 film, *Southern Comfort*, a Cajun version of *Deliverance*. I could almost hear "Dueling Accordions" wailing off in the distance.

I tried to call the school, but there was no reception. And, I couldn't exactly consult WAZE since the app, or apps for that matter, didn't exist yet.

When I finally reached Franklin, I was a good 45 minutes late. Entering the auditorium, I felt like Roger Moore on that tiny island in the alligator scene from *Live and Let Die*. I was in hostile territory. And, I didn't have any cool gadgets from Q.

Like Alexander at Issus or Nelson at Trafalgar, I needed a **bold** plan. I would kick off the show with a riveting story that ended with a smashing crescendo. I would then facilitate a number of engaging, real-world activities, shower the crowd with resources and SWAG like Mardi Gras beads from Endymion, and then, for my coup de grâce, serve up boiled crawfish from New Iberia!

It was a fine plan! Definitely **bold**. But, alas, my coup de grâce got delivered prematurely…

When doing presentations, I always used a yellow Whiffle bat as a pointer. It was eye-catching, light, and fun to wield around like a sword. And, when I rapped it against a blackboard, or even a child's head, it made a loud noise, but didn't cause any significant damage.

Two minutes into my monologue, I came to the painful realization that my riveting story was anything but *riveting*. Peering into the audience, I noticed the Assistant Principal reading *USA Today*, several teachers playing solitaire on their laptops, and two coaches in the back loudly de-

Delivering a workshop in 2010

bating the Saints' recent draft choices. So, I skipped ahead to my smashing crescendo.

I landed the punch line with an awkward pirouette, yelled the Cajun version of the cowboy, "Yee-haw!" "Ayeee!" and then slammed my Whiffle bat against an empty desk in the front row. There was a thunderous "Crack!" "If my audience hadn't been paying attention before," I thought, "it certainly would be now!"

It was.

When the bat hit the table, all heads popped up from their sundry, non-workshop-related tasks and glared at me through bulging eyes.

All but one, that is. A large, older woman in the second row craned her head toward the ceiling instead. She clutched her chest, gasped for breath, tipped over backwards in her chair, and collapsed on the floor like a sack of oysters. The audience shrieked, looked at the woman with concern, and then back at me with scorn.

I was the actor, John Wilkes Booth at Ford's Theatre, only there was nowhere to jump!

As the paramedics carted the woman off on a gurney, the principal pulled me aside and said, "Mr. Dunbar, I think we're done for the day."

I looked down and shook my head in agreement.

I called to cancel the crawfish order, loaded up the car with bags of undistributed SWAG, and headed back across the Atchafalaya. The fog had lifted; the traffic was light.

———

Postmortem: I am happy/relieved to report that the woman survived. She and the school both eventually recovered from the ordeal—without my assistance I might add. As for me, I traded in my Whiffle bat for a Nerf sword. "*En garde*!"

Something
About New Orleans

My wife and I have left New Orleans a number of times. Going against the practical advice and desperate pleas of family and friends and probably defying logic, we've always returned. It would be easy (and a bit cliché) to say it was the music, food, or architecture that drew us back. Truth is, it was something else.

What, pray tell? I'm not exactly sure. My mother, a character culled from the pages of a Tennessee Williams play, used to blame it on some unexplainable ethereal force. "Even Marie Laveau," she would say, "couldn't peg a voodoo pin to it." My father, the quintessential *southern gentleman* says, "The city is like an old familiar chicken coop. Eventually, we all come back to roost." My doctor diagnosed it as "dementia induced by the balmy subtropical heat." We were incapable of responsible decision-making because our gray matter had been reduced to a lumpy, swamp-like roux. A lay meteorologist friend of mine quickly retorted, "It's not the heat, it's the humidity stupid." Another friend of mine is an entomologist. For him, the answer was easy: "The place is just crawling with bugs. Swarming termites and marauding fire ants, cockroaches the size of pterodactyls, and mosquitoes capable of carrying off small bovine, what's not to like?" And then

New Orleans rising from the fog

there are the transplants, people who came down for Jazz
Fest or Mardi Gras and never left. While dancing to the
Iguanas at Café Brazil or drinking a Pimm's Cup at the
Napoleon House, they slammed headlong into their geo-
graphical soul mate. It's as if they were abducted by aliens,
aliens who just happen to live on a much cooler planet.
(Dorothy, you're definitely not in Kansas anymore!) They
buy a shotgun double and rent out the other half, take a
few classes at Tulane or UNO, acquire a taste for chicory
and seersucker, and, eventually, join the "confederacy of
dunces." Like so many other Big Queasy "char-ac-tuz"
(listen to Dr. John's rendition of "Basin Street Blues" for
the proper pronunciation), they become part of the ethereal force my mom couldn't quite put a finger on.

Two days before Katrina hit, my wife and I fled to the
"high ground" of Avery Island. We watched from a distance in disbelief as our city was battered and beaten about.
We, like others around the world, were incensed by the slow
response and human folly of it all. It was utterly surreal.

For the longest time, we considered leaving. San Fran-

Mobile homes on rail cars being brought to NOLA after Katrina. (2005)

cisco, Charleston, Key West, Charlottesville, and a slough of European and Latin American cities made the initial cut. We listened to people far more rational than us, and we swallowed the poison of one pragmatic argument after another. And then, two days before the mayor said we could return, we were back.

When people ask me what it is that keeps us here, I think of George Harrison's famous song and simply say, "Something."

You Belong to Me, A Prospect One art installation after Hurricane Katrina

Objects of Attachment
That Hold Us Together

My wife and I packed a couple of small bags, loaded our boxer, Boudin, into the backseat, and headed West— out of the path of the approaching storm. Just like the summer before, and the time before that, we figured we would be gone for no more than a day or two. We'd return, clean up, and get back to "normal."

But this time was different.

We spent the next two and a half months in Avery Island, Lafayette, Houston, Birmingham, and Chapel Hill. Along with thousands of others, we were Katrina refugees.

During our "hurrication," we drank a lot of wine— first the good stuff, and then whatever box or jug we could get our hands on. We became situational alcoholics, as in, "This situation sucks—I need a drink!"

We also had a number of fierce conversations. We talked about the failings of the Army Corps of Engineers and our fine politicians, the inevitable consequences of climate change for a low-lying region like ours, and, the possibility of rebuilding a better, safer, and (hopefully) smarter New Orleans. We debated who among our friends would stay and who would leave. And, we talked about the things we left behind—those things that might not be there when we returned.

Of course, everybody mentioned photographs. "Family albums, and the memories they invoke are impossible to replace," we all agreed.

"But what about the other stuff?" a friend asked. "If you could have only taken three additional items, what would they have been?"

"That's easy," I said, "my camel bell, watch, and santo."

The Camel Bell

Near the end of my junior year in college, my father's land development business imploded. The real-estate market collapsed and interest rates skyrocketed. He ended up spending almost everything he had, including paintings, servicing debts and bailing out partners. As a result, he wasn't able to help me out with my tuition. I had an athletic scholarship and a couple of jobs at the time, but there was no way I could cover the cost. So, I applied for a student loan, and I decided to withdraw for at least a semester in order to save money.

That summer, I went to visit my great aunt, Anina Terrel. She was one of my favorite people on the plan-
et. She was an amazing
woman. She had been
on the first ocean liner to
pass through the Panama
Canal, she had driven an
ambulance in World War
I, she had crossed Afri-
ca from Cairo to Cape

Town on horses, camels, trains and steamships, and she had owned and managed a ranch in Colorado. "Aunt Anini," as we called her, lived to be 103.

She was also a great storyteller. (She certainly had plenty of material.) When I arrived at her apartment, she launched into one of her many tales about her travels in China, her favorite country.

"So, there I was on the Great Wall of China," she said. "A tremendous camel train appeared off in the distance. As it approached, our entire party was swallowed up by a massive cloud of dust. When it finally settled, I looked down and noticed an old bronze bell swinging from the neck of the lead camel. I turned to my husband and said, 'Roy, I want that bell. I have to have it!'

"Roy looked at me as though I was crazy, but, of course, he knew I wasn't. I always got what I wanted.

"He asked our guide to barter for the bell. After a lively exchange, the guide tossed down a few coins, and the camel-puller cut the bell from the animal's neck and tossed it up. That was around 1937 I believe. Your father must have been about ten years old at the time."

Aunt Anini then reached into a desk drawer and pulled out the bronze bell. "I want you to have this," she said. "And, I want you to see the world like I did. Travel is truly the world's greatest teacher." She paused to let me think about it.

"But first," she continued, "I need for you to finish your formal education here." She reached into her purse and handed me a check—and winked.

After graduating from Duke University in May of the following year, I joined the Peace Corps and moved to

Ecuador. There, I would continue my education with "the
world's greatest teacher."

Aunt Anini, as always, got what she wanted.

The Watch

My mom lived in a tiny three-room apartment in the
Lower Garden District. She didn't have a lot of stuff, but
what she did have, barely fit. There were paintings by my
dad leaning against the wall; she had a collection of ash-
trays she had "borrowed" from restaurants and hotels;
colonial santos, milagro crosses, and other collectibles
from Mexico crowded the tables; and her dishwasher was
overflowing with items that were definitely not dishes. Her
place looked like a funky old antique shop on Magazine
Street.

One day I stopped by for a quick visit, and my mom
immediately launched into an impassioned sales pitch:
"Darling," she said, "you just have to take some of this
clutter off my hands! This place is a wreck—I can't bear it
any longer! Whatever you want, it's yours!"

"I'm good," I said. "My place is actually smaller than
yours. And, besides, I don't really need anything."

"I didn't ask what you need darling," she said. "I asked
you what you want. You know, I'm not gonna live forever."

"That's a rather morbid thing to say," I said. "You're
only sixty-two. I'd prefer you stick around for a while."

"I'll try," she said, "but, I am feeling rather ill." She
coughed, held the back of her hand to her forehead, and
pretended to faint.

"OK mom," I said, "you win. You can leave me the

watch in your will."

My mom wore a men's Tiffany watch. It was stainless steel with a large white face and black Roman numerals. She wore it on her right wrist, below a long stack of bracelets that almost covered her entire arm.

"Yes," I said, "the watch is all I want."

About a month later, I celebrated my thirtieth birthday with my family and future wife. After dinner, there were a few toasts, and, we all enjoyed a Doberge cake from Gambino's Bakery. Then, my mom clinked her glass with a spoon, a little too loudly as always, and slid a small box across the table. I instantly knew what it was—and, I suspected what it might mean.

When I opened the box, I found that the watch was set to the day and hour I was born. My mom and I both smiled—and then cried.

My mother died four months later from complications due to ovarian cancer. To her wishes, we scattered her

ashes beneath a magnolia tree in Jackson Square, attended mass at Saint Louis Cathedral, and then had lunch at
Galatoire's on her. I wore the watch.

The Santo

My mother and father loved Mexico. They traveled to
the country almost every other year. They would sometimes visit the famous New Orleans sculptor, Enrique
Alférez, who had a home and studio in Morelia. On one
such trip, I was actually conceived.

As an artist, my father was inspired by the paintings
and architecture of colonial cities like Cuernavaca, Guadalajara, and Mérida. He especially admired the gilded
ceilings and picture frames found in the ornate baroque
churches. Over the years, my dad mastered the techniques
used to create them, and he began to incorporate them
into his own unique works of contemporary art.

My mother was more of a shopper. She bought silver
jewelry from Taxco, pottery from Jalisco, and rugs and
blankets from Oaxaca. And, she was always on the hunt
for colonial santos. Santos are carved wooden or ivory figures usually depicting saints or angels. They can be found
in the niches and alters of churches, convents, and monas-
teries throughout Latin America and the Philippines. My
mom ended up with a huge collection.

With their marble eyes and missing limbs, most of the
santos in our house scared me. They looked like possessed
dolls from a horror film.

All but one, that is.

There was a small boy about a foot tall with an angelic face and piercing eyes. Possibly a young Saint Jude, the patron saint of lost causes, it had three small flames shooting from its head. To me, it was like Leonardo da Vinci's *Vitruvian Man*; it was perfect. Created by some long-forgotten artisan, it was simple yet elegant, delicate yet strong. It reminded me of the statue of David by Alférez on Poydras Street in New Orleans; it was proud and defiant.

When my mom died, she left the little santo to me. It now resides in our living room, in the center of a fireplace mantle.

The summer after I lost my mother, my future wife and I took our first trip together as a couple. For reasons I couldn't explain, we went to Mexico. We visited Querétaro, Guanajuato, and San Miguel de Allende. It was an emotional and unforgettable trip. Over the years, we returned to the country no fewer than twenty times. We hurled ourselves into the mosh pit of Mexico City's buses and subways, we sipped smoky mezcal in Oaxaca, a city with a name you have to spit, we toured ruined henequen haciendas and bathed in sapphire-blue cenotes in the Yucatán, we battled Montezuma (and perhaps Maximilian I) in Puebla, we tested the marriage on the Volcano of Fire, and we survived (just barely) a most memorable night in a palapa in Yelapa. Like my parents, we fell in love with the country—so much so that we even named our new dog, "Mole," after the sauce and not the rodent of course.

Today, whenever I pass through our living room, I always steal a glance at the little figure on the mantle. I think about our next excursion south of the border; I think about my parents and their (our) love affair with Mexico; I think about my own "concepción inmaculada"; and, I think about the objects of attachment that bind us together.

———

Author's Note: Our house didn't flood in Katrina. We were lucky. This article is dedicated to the people who weren't as fortunate—those who lost photographs and other objects of attachment.

The Fall Guy
*How I Lost my Job and
Rediscovered my Calling*

I was at a market in Antigua, Guatemala. A song with an upbeat tempo came on the radio. I started tapping my feet. Soon, I was dancing and singing in the aisles. Locals assumed I was just a crazy *extranjero*. They didn't realize what I had been through. My wife turned to our friends and said, "He's back. My husband is back!"

My Calling

Like most teachers, I went into the profession because of my experiences as a student. I loved to learn, I had great teachers and coaches, and every day in the classroom had been an adventure.

I went on to teach everything from small animal husbandry and first grade to middle school geography and AP US History. I also coached football, tennis, and wrestling. I once confessed to parents at an open house, "I can't believe they actually pay me to do this. It's too much fun!"

After about a decade in the classroom though, I became restless. I wanted to do more; I wanted to have a bigger impact on a greater number of kids. Teaching teachers seemed a logical next step.

With my students at Young Audiences Charter School

So, I took a position with a group out of Cambridge, Massachusetts, that was trying to reinvent public education. We developed a comprehensive reform model and tried it out with struggling schools around the country. I did professional development on whole-school change, project-based teaching and learning, arts integration, team-based school organization, curriculum alignment, and the effective use of instructional technology. It was like Peace Corps with a paycheck.

When Hurricane Katrina hit, I was working with schools in far-flung places like Soldotna, Alaska, and the Pine Ridge Indian Reservation in South Dakota. I wanted to help rebuild schools in my own community; I wanted to be part of the recovery.

I applied for a number of jobs and eventually landed a position with the Louisiana Department of Education (LDOE). I became the state's Academic Advisor for Charter Schools. I recruited and evaluated potential charter school operators; I did workshops for aspiring school leaders and board members; and I conducted quality reviews of existing schools. It was about as far from the classroom as I had ever been. And, unlike teaching, it wasn't much fun! Nonetheless, I thought I could make a difference…

With my students at Young Audiences Charter School in Gretna, La.

The Bribe

One of the first schools I reviewed was a New Orleans charter that wanted to open up a second campus in Baton Rouge. Along with a group of seasoned educators, I found a number of glaring deficiencies. I recommended that the state not approve the application. Unfortunately, they ignored my advice and approved the charter anyway.

A few months later, teachers at the original school complained to the Recovery School District (RSD) and the LDOE. I met with the teachers and listened to their concerns. Afterward, I suggested that the state conduct a formal investigation. I assembled a team of experienced educators with no connections to the school or district, and I drafted a protocol for the inspection.

When we arrived at the school, we saw a line of buses pulling out of the parking lot. It wasn't on the schedule, but apparently half the school was going on a field trip. It was the first of many bizarre discoveries.

Our team observed the remaining classes, reviewed documents and artifacts, and interviewed teachers and students. At the end of the day, we met and compared notes. The team validated the teachers' earlier concerns and uncovered several others. They included inadequate services for students with special needs, staff doing science fair projects for students, a class that hadn't had a teacher for most of the year, complaints about teachers who couldn't speak English, adults using racial epithets, forged documents, prayer rugs, and unopened resources purchased with public funds. The team was disturbed by the findings.

Because of the field trip, I scheduled a follow-up visit. During that inspection, I was unexpectedly called into the principal's office. There, I was confronted by a group that included board members from the school, staff from the charter school management organization or CMO, faculty from Louisiana State University, and, strangest of all, representatives from a construction company in Texas. The VP of the company was an attractive young woman from Turkey. The group showered me with compliments, many of which I certainly didn't deserve. They told me that the school was in trouble and that it needed my help. I told them that I was there simply to collect information. I would provide that information to the state, and the LDOE would then decide next steps.

Before we left, the young woman from the construction company pulled me aside and asked if she could meet with me "in private" later that night. I declined. She then called me at home and begged me to meet with her the following day. She said it was "absolutely imperative." I checked with my boss. Curious, he thought it might be a good idea. He cautioned, "Just make sure it's in a public space, and that you take good notes."

We met at coffee shop on Magazine Street in New Orleans. Again, she showered me with compliments. She told me that I "was the only one who could save the school." I told her it was not my job to save the school. I said I was there simply to make sure that the school had fulfilled its charter, that it was in compliance with state law, and that the kids were safe. Obviously frustrated, she turned to me and said, "Mr. Dunbar, I have $25,000 to make this problem go away, twenty for you and five for me." Dumfounded, I told her it would be unethical for me to accept money from the school. She stormed out the coffee shop, jumped into a rental car, and drove away. I never saw her again.

I immediately wrote down a detailed account of what had happened. I shared it with my boss and then met with a lawyer from the LDOE. He suggested that I tell the police department, which I did. The police told me there was nothing they could do. According to them, there was not enough evidence. They needed eyewitnesses or a recording.

In my report to the LDOE, I recommended that the charter be revoked, and that the RSD run the school until a new operator could be found. I also suggested that they hire more people to monitor schools. At the time, I was the only one in the state. My recommendations were dismissed. (In retrospect, I think the state didn't want the bad press.) Instead, they asked me to create a Corrective Action Plan for the school, which I did.

"This is a time bomb," I told a colleague. "Sooner or later, it's gonna explode."

"And you'll be collateral damage," she said.

After the experience, I started looking for a new job. I had definitely strayed far from my calling. Unfortunately, I didn't find one in time.

Under the Bus

After the incident with the disgruntled teachers, I recommended to the LDOE that it adopt a formal whistleblower policy. Instead, it had an intern create a protocol for complaints. The protocol involved going to the principal, going to the school's board, and then filling out an online form that was sent to the state.

A young teacher at the school who was trying desperately to save her job had a grievance, but she ignored the new protocol. Instead of going to the board, she went to the press. The press did a records request, and voilà, all of my reports hit the fan! The teacher's allegations couldn't be substantiated, but the ones they dredged up could. It ignited, for lack of a better expression, a shit storm.

The next morning, I was on the cover of the local paper. They were calling me a "whistleblower." Actually, the real whistleblowers had been the teachers who originally came forward—and who were inevitably fired.

The LDOE scrambled to do damage control. They told me not to talk to the press, and ordered me to come to Baton Rouge to meet with a PR specialist. The meeting never happened though. Instead, I got a phone call telling me "my services were no longer needed." I was not given an explanation, nor was I given an opportunity to defend myself. I was a casualty of Louisiana politics; I was "the fall guy."

The next day I was on the cover of the local paper again. This time the heading read: "Whistleblower Fired."

I was in shock. "Things like this don't happen in education," I thought.

I was wrong.

Friends and colleagues told me not to worry. They said everything would be OK.

As it turns out, I had reason to be concerned. The organization that ran the school had ties to countless schools and businesses in other states and countries. There was also an alleged connection to a powerful imam living in exile in the United States. There was a lot at stake—far more than 25k! I got calls from *The New York Times* and *60 Minutes*. It was crazy; it was surreal.

Thrown under the (school) bus by my employer, I was now left alone to face the consequences.

I couldn't sleep at night. I was paralyzed by anxiety. I found myself checking under my car for bombs and looking over my shoulder for "suspicious characters." "Destroyer" by the Kinks kept playing in my head:

> Doctor, doctor, help me please, I know you'll understand
>
> There's a time device inside of me, I'm a self-destructin' man
>
> There's a red, under my bed
>
> And there's a little green man in my head
>
> And he said, you're not goin' crazy, you're just a bit sad
>
> 'Cause there's a man in ya, gnawin' ya, tearin' ya into two.
>
> Silly boy, you self-destroyer.
>
> Paranoia, the destroyer

One afternoon, a neighbor stopped me on the street. He said, "Dude, what the fuck's going on? The FBI was snooping around your house. Are you in trouble?"

"I'm not sure," I said.

The next day I got a lawyer and called the FBI to set up a meeting. They questioned me under oath for more than three hours. When they finished, I asked them if I had done anything wrong. They said, "No, we just wish you had come to us first. You should never have gone to the police. We could have actually done something about this. Now, it's probably too late." I then asked if my family was safe. They confessed, "We don't know."

Friends and colleagues from around the country came to my rescue. They invited me to visit—to escape the madness. Two of our friends had recently retired to Antigua, Guatemala. When I got an email inviting us to come down, I wrote, "¡*Sí, porqué no*! Yes, why not?!"

The Sanctuary

Three volcanoes loom over Antigua. One constantly coughs up smoke, another occasionally spits out fire, and a third just grumbles. The city is a time capsule. In 1773, it was completely destroyed by an earthquake. Three years later, the Spanish government relocated the capital to a safer location. The people were ordered to leave, but many refused. They stayed and just lived among the ruins. Like diehard residents of New Orleans after Katrina (myself included), they could never abandon the home they loved. Today, Antigua is hauntingly beautiful.

Guatemala reminded me of Ecuador, where I had been a Peace Corps volunteer many years before. It was there that I first started teaching; it was there that I discovered my calling.

At a market near the main square, a song came on the radio. I started tapping my feet—and smiled for the first time in several months.

Smiling in Antigua, Guatemala
(2011)

Epilogue

A year and a half after
I had made my recom-
mendation to revoke the
charter, the school was
finally shut down. (At the
time, it was actually in compliance with all of the measures in my Corrective Action Plan.) The other school
that I had recommended not be given a charter was also
eventually closed. It was cold comfort, but I felt somewhat
vindicated.

I wrote down a list of all of the lessons I had learned
from the experience. I'd share them here, but they are not
all politically correct, and a few are not even "SFW." Suffice it to say, I've taken them all to heart.

When I returned from Guatemala, I started working
with schools around the country. I did quality reviews and
helped faculty and staff identify strengths and challenges.
I also did professional development for teachers and wrote
articles about instructional "best practices." Eventually, I
partnered with a local nonprofit and opened up a school
that integrated the arts across the curriculum. Each day,
I greeted the kids with a hug, a handshake, a high five, or
a song. In education, it's the little things that matter most!

I was also inspired, no, compelled to write down all my
survival tales.

A Bad Diagnosis
*Surviving a handful of
lesions on my left lung*

When I turned thirty-five, my wife insisted that I get a physical. I told her I was fine and didn't need one, but she was persistent. "It's better to be safe than sorry," she said.

Soon, I would come to loathe that expression.

At the hospital, they drew blood, checked my vitals, took chest X-rays, and had me fill out a lengthy questionnaire. My doctor then gave me the dreaded prostate exam. (FYI: When choosing a physician, always take into consideration finger size!) Removing his gloves, he said, "So, Mr. Dunbar, it says here you eat a lot of boudin and cracklin. I don't have the results yet, but I am a little concerned about your cholesterol. Diet aside, you seem to be the picture of health. I think you're good to go. Tell your wife you don't have to come back for another five years!"

As I skipped toward my car, a nurse ran up behind me in a panic. "I'm sorry Mr. Dunbar, but the doctor needs to see you again."

"Hmmmm," I thought. "Am I safe or sorry?"

When I stepped into his office, he and three other doctors were huddled around a glowing screen. "Did you ever smoke?" one of them asked.

"No," I replied.

"Hmmmm," he said.

195

"We discovered something on the plain films," my doctor said.

"What's a plain film?" I asked.

"Sorry, I mean X-rays," he clarified. "We found five lesions on your left lung."

My heart, a neighboring organ, skipped a beat. I looked up at the screen, and sure enough there were five dark splotches. One was as big as a quarter, and the other four were about the size of a dime. "What is it?" I asked.

"Well, it's probably one of two things," my doctor said. "The most obvious of course is cancer. Though it's unusual since you never smoked."

"The second possibility," he said with a morose hint of excitement in his voice, "is a tropical fungus. You told me you lived in South America—there's a chance you could have picked it up down there. We haven't seen a case in the States in years."

"Is the prognosis better than cancer?" I asked.

"Not so much," he said. "It's usually fatal, but there are some promising treatments."

I was starting to question my doctor's bedside manner.

"I'm ordering a number of tests," he said, "including a CT scan and some additional blood work. We'll talk about next steps on Monday. Until then, just sit tight."

"Right?!" I thought. It was only Wednesday.

When I told my wife, she burst into tears. I tried to console her by telling her that *she* would be fine. "You're still young and attractive," I said. "You'll have no trouble finding someone else, preferably someone who makes more money than a teacher. I am concerned about our sweet boxer, Hola, though. I got her before we met, and y'all haven't exactly bonded. I might need for you to put her down and bury her next to me."

"*Our* dog Hola is a whore for kibble," she said. "I'll give her some Alpo and a pig ear, and she'll be just fine."

Humor is definitely the ultimate placebo!

I had a copy of the "plain films" sent to a good friend of mine who's a doctor in North Carolina. "I don't like either diagnosis—it doesn't make sense," he said. "I really want to see the results from that CT scan. Send them my way as soon as ya can." (He later confessed that he thought I was toast!)

On Thursday, I flew to Miami to do a presentation for teachers. During my session, I started coughing uncontrollably. I felt like I had a python from the Everglades wrapped around my chest. By the time I got back to New Orleans, I could hardly breathe.

On Friday, I had a CT scan of my entire upper body. That night, I discovered blood in my urine. Whatever I had was advancing quickly. When I informed my doctor, he told me that he wasn't surprised. "We'll discuss treatment options next week."

When I told my dad, he and I both broke down. Telling a loved one about a serious illness is often worse than the actual illness.

Over the weekend, my wife and I had a number of heart-to-hearts. "Depending on my condition," I said, "I'd really like to see a few places before I die." I mentioned New Zealand, the Serengeti, Istanbul, and Prague. "I wouldn't mind spending my last days in the Greek Isles," I said. I then told her I wanted to be cremated—along with Hola—and have my ashes tossed in the bayou near my childhood home.

"I'll do whatever you want," she said.

When I met with the doctor on Monday, he seemed nervous. He squirmed in his seat as he spoke. (In retrospect, I think he was worried about a lawsuit.) "I've got really good news Mr. Dunbar," he said. "The results from the other tests were all negative. You don't have cancer. Or the tropical fungus from South America."

"But what about the coughing and blood?" I asked.

"I think you may have picked up the flu," he said. "It's just a coincidence. And the blood was probably a bad reaction to the CT scan. You'll be fine."

"And the lesions?" I asked.

"Well, um, a," he stammered. "We believe the technician may have mishandled your prints. The splotches were most likely her fingers."

"So, it was just a bad diagnosis," I said. I drew in a deep breath, coughed—and then smiled!

The Nightmare at Dreams

*A Family's Misadventures
on the Mayan Riviera*

"It's all about the kids," my father reminded me for the eighty-third time. "I want to make sure my grandchildren have a good time. I need for you to be their camp counselor."

"I know Dad," I said. "I've got it covered."

My father was taking us on a family vacation. He wanted my brother and me to "bond" with our niece, Hali James, and our nephew, Dunbar, aka, Gator. They lived with my sister and her husband in Colorado at the time, and we hadn't seen them in almost a year.

My sister was given the task of finding the "perfect" destination. After extensive research, she settled on Dreams, an all-inclusive, kid-friendly resort just north of the Mayan ruins of Tulum. It had a water slide, parasailing, a jump house, a life-size chess set, a climbing wall, and several kiddie pools. It also had five all-you-can-eat theme-based buffets and "exciting planned activities for the entire family." It was basically a landlocked Disney cruise ship, i.e., purgatory for anyone older than twelve.

The night before the trip, as if taking laxatives for a colonoscopy, my wife and I reluctantly and hastily packed for an early morning departure. Somehow, in our reluctance and haste, we failed to pack our passports, a revelation we wouldn't have until we reached Louis Armstrong International Airport an hour and a half before our flight.

"You've got to be kidding me!" I screamed.

"No," my wife said, "I think they're on the kitchen table."

She jumped out of the car; I cursed, pounded the steering wheel and turned around. There was at least an outside chance I could make it back in time.

Driving like a typical New Orleans commuter, I zigzagged in and out of traffic, blew past police cars and ambulances, sailed through stop signs and red lights, and Knieveled over cavernous potholes and miscellaneous road debris.

Returning to the airport in record time, I pulled into the short-term parking lot like a NASCAR pit stop. Grabbing my ticket, I suddenly noticed an orange light flashing, "Full!" I cursed, pounded the steering wheel, shifted into reverse, stepped on the gas and—slammed into an embankment. It ripped off my side view mirror, bumper, and right front tire. I cursed, pounded the already battered steering wheel, and then rode the rim slowly toward long-term parking.

I found the last spot on the top floor, and took off like OJ Simpson in a 1970s Hertz commercial (not to be confused with his infamous Bronco run from the law thirty years later). I raced across the airport, hurdling bags, dodging passengers, and pushing aside old ladies and small children. When I arrived at security, out of breath and, apparently, time, my wife just shrugged and shook her head.

"You've got to be kidding me?" I said.

"No," she replied. "They just closed the gate."

I then turned around and saw my brother and his girl-friend walking in through the door. "What the &%$!" I yelled.

"We over-slept," my brother casually confessed.

"You've GOT to be kidding me?!" I barked.

"No," he said, "we were really tired."

At that exact moment, my cell phone rang. When I answered, I could feel tears gurgling up from the earpiece. "My passport expired!" my sister wailed. "They won't let us on the plane."

"YOU'VE GOT TO BE KIDDING ME?!" I screamed.

"No," she cried. "It's gonna take days to get a new one. We can't go to Mexico!"

Like a scene from a Spaghetti Western, I looked at my brother, my brother looked at my wife, my wife looked at his girlfriend, and she looked at me. Then, we all stared at the floor in disbelief. "Holy crap!" I said, "we're the &%*$ing Griswolds!"

Somewhere over the Atchafalaya swamp in a Boeing 737, my dad was craning his neck to see where we were. His wife, a bit more suspicious, just scowled.

We immediately put ourselves on the standby list for the next overbooked flight to Houston. But, our prospects looked grim.

Then, unexpectedly, Fortuna smiled on our little "con-federacy of dunces." It was the day after Mardi Gras and a number of passengers, obviously hungover, missed the flight. We, miraculously, just barely made the cut.

Pushed by an unusual tailwind, we arrived in Houston

ten minutes early and made our connection with only seconds to spare.

We didn't tell my dad what had happened because we were too embarrassed; he didn't ask because he was too proud. His wife shot us a knowing glance and then buried her disgust in a crossword puzzle from *The New York Times*.

We also didn't tell my father about the passport fiasco in Colorado. My sister, who was supposed to arrive later that day, would have to deliver that time bomb herself.

In Cancun, we picked up a large van with two child seats and drove toward Dreams.

When we passed a sign for "Cenotes," natural freshwater pools, my dad said, "Ya know, Gator and Hali James are gonna love swimming in cenotes!"

When we passed a sign for "Stingray Alley," he said, "Ya know, Gator and Hali James are gonna love swimming with stingrays."

Signs for zip-lines, the ancient ruins of Coba, and an assortment of unpronounceable Mayan diversions all starting with "X," were followed by similar pronouncements.

After each one, we all squirmed in awkward silence.

At Dreams, my father finally received the dreaded call from my sister. From that moment forward, crestfallen yet stoic, my father replaced the future tense with the conditional perfect: "Gator and Hali James would have really enjoyed parasailing. Gator and Hali James would have loved the water slide."

For the next five days, my dad and his wife read books on the beach, trying desperately to ignore the peals of laughter from other people's grandchildren. As for us, we

My wife and I in Mexico

escaped the Disney compound whenever we could, and we took tremendous solace in the resort's all-you-can-drink frozen mojito machine.

Our time in Tulum would forever be remembered as, "The Nightmare at Dreams."

———

Author's Note: Whenever my sister criticizes me for doing something wrong, I simply remind her of Dreams.

This summer, our family is finally attempting another trip. It's been years since the train wreck in Tulum, but the PTSD still lingers.

A Walk in the Woods
Above Lake Atitlán

Note: I recently read Bill Bryson's celebrated book, *A Walk in the Woods: Rediscovering America on the Appalachian Trail*. (It's much better than the film by the way.) In it, the author discovers the power and majesty of nature and his own physical and mental limitations. During a much shorter hike in Guatemala, I had similar revelations. While they weren't as profound, they were painfully earned and certainly memorable!

———

It was the summer of 1995. I was staying at a hostel in San Pedro La Laguna on Lake Atitlán in Guatamala. I had been trekking alone for two weeks; I was hoping to find some traveling companions in town. At a café on the main square, I met a group from the Netherlands that was heading in the same direction. I asked them if they wanted to go for a hike.

"No, I think we're just gonna relax by the lake," they said. "Why don't we get together for Happy Hour?"

"Sounds like a plan," I said. I finished my coffee and set out for the woods.

I was wearing shorts, a t-shirt and a pair of Tevas. I had a bottle of flat orange Fanta and a few *quetzals*, the local currency in my pocket. A didn't have a map, a compass or a smartphone (it hadn't been invented yet). I didn't carry a daypack because, well, I didn't have anything to carry. And, besides, I'd only be gone a few hours. Or so I thought.

I picked up a skinny trail on the edge of the lake. It wound its way up toward an imposing volcano high above town. The woods were thick and the climb was steep.

After about an hour and a half, I saw what appeared to be a harpy eagle, the largest raptor in the Americas. I was excited. I had never seen one before. Without binoculars though, I wasn't able to verify the sighting. My birder buddies back in the states would have had their doubts. So, I left the path to get a closer look.

In retrospect, this was probably a mistake. I should have remembered a pivotal scene from one of my favorite films, *An American Werewolf in London*. In it, the two protagonists are warned repeatedly to "stay on the road" and "keep clear of the moors." They don't. One gets eaten and the other starts howling at the moon.

I followed the bird deep into the jungle. Every time I got close, it would fly off to a more distant tree.

Finally, I came to a small clearing on the edge of a deep ravine. I couldn't go any farther. I stood up on my tiptoes and craned my neck to catch a final, definitive glimpse of the elusive bird. Then, all of a sudden, my foot exploded. It felt like my big toe had been dipped in acid. I shrieked like an eagle, and the eagle flew off for good.

Looking down to see if my toe was still attached, I saw a big bright, furry velvet ant smiling up at me. There was blood, my blood, gleaming from its gaster.

According to the entomologist Dr. Justin O. Schmidt, the velvet ant sting is a solid "3" on his infamous pain index. He describes it as "explosive and long lasting; you sound insane as you scream. Hot oil from the deep fryer spilling all over your entire foot." Yep, that's pretty much how it felt.

Within minutes, my toe grew to the size (and color) of a Red Delicious apple. It throbbed like a second heart. Not having a companion to point out the obvious, that it wouldn't have happened if I had been wearing proper shoes, I thought to myself, "It's a good thing I'm in sandals. My big big toe wouldn't fit in hiking boots."

Limping back toward the path, I became disoriented. Everything in the jungle looked the same. And, there was no harpy eagle to guide me back. So, I plodded along—in a general direction.

After about an hour, I stumbled upon what I thought was the original path. (It wasn't!)

Then, as if on the biblical Job's cue, it started to rain. Buckets of rain! Within seconds, the skinny trail turned into a broad, muddy raging river. Following my questionable intuition (and the current), I headed off in a direction I hoped would take me back to town.

It didn't. Instead, it took me to a small Mayan village where a family, seeing my deformed toe and lack of provisions, offered me shelter from the storm. I told them I was trying to get back to San Pedro, but apparently, they didn't speak Spanish. They spoke Tz'utujil, a Mayan language I couldn't understand, pronounce, or spell.

So, we sat on the floor of the family's tiny thatched hut in silence. They served me handmade corn tortillas, *Poc*

Chuc (a slow cooked pork), black beans, "dog snout" salsa, and *horchata*, a blend of rice milk, ground almonds, cinnamon, and sugar. The food was delicious and the scene was surreal.

When the rain finally stopped, I tried to give the good Samaritans all my soggy quetzals. But, they declined. They figured I needed the money more than they did. Using gestures, I thanked them for their hospitality and headed back down the muddy trail.

After about a mile or two, I stopped to reconnoiter, only to realize I didn't know what the word meant. So, I continued on.

Around midafternoon, I came to a footbridge over a small creek, where I met a farmer who spoke broken Spanish. When I asked him for directions to San Pedro, he gave me a look that said, "How the &%$# did you end up here you boneheaded gringo!?" He told me I was walking in the wrong direction and that San Pedro was many hours away. "*Vaya con Dios y suerte*!" he said as he left me on the bridge. "Go with God and luck" didn't sound all that encouraging. I wasn't keen on the idea of backtracking either (nor missing Happy Hour). So, I came up with an alternate plan—kinda like Napoleon's decision to invade Russia.

I was teaching middle school social studies at the time. Because of this, I knew very well that all streams and rivers ran downhill. And, unlike manmade trails that followed the contour of the surrounding hills, they usually took a more direct, expedited path. I also knew that rivers were tributaries and that tributaries usually emptied into larger bodies of water, like, say, lakes for example. San

Pedro was on a lake, hence "La Laguna." I figured if I followed the stream down the mountain, I'd be sipping a margarita with my new Dutch friends in no time at all. Or so I thought.

The rocks were slick and the current was strong. As I slipped, tripped, and stumbled my way down, *the little stream that could* (possibly take me home) swelled to the size of a whitewater river with Class VI rapids.

At some point along the way, dying of thirst, I decided to drink from those rapids. Two days later in a public restroom in Chichicastenango, I came to regret that decision—again and again!

The first waterfall I encountered was small enough to slide down. The second and third were much bigger. I had to hack my way around them. The fourth was an absolute beast! It bellowed like wolves from the underworld and it coughed up a vast, blinding mist. It was the mother, father, grandparents, and extended family of all falls. Without a barrel or luck, two things I definitely didn't have at the time, there was no way I was going over. Once again, I'd have to plow my way around—way around.

After only a few steps into my detour, I slipped and fell. Like Michael Douglas in *Romancing the Stone* (without the benefit of having Kathleen Turner to land on), I shot down a muddy flume at breakneck speed. Just before sailing off into the abyss, I latched on to an exposed root and clod of firm clay. On a thin ledge over a bottomless, rocky gorge, I came to a precarious stop.

There, paralyzed by fear and exhaustion, I weighed my flimsy options. I figured I had three. One was to shelter in place, scream, "¡*Ayuda*!" or "Help!" every few minutes, and hope that someone would eventually come to my rescue. It was unlikely but possible. Another was to clamber back up the steep ravine in the dark and take the long trail back to town. I figured my odds were about as good as those of the Uruguayan rugby team that crashed in the Andes in 1972. The third was to jump. If I hit enough trees on the way down, I'd potentially survive the fall. I'd seen it done in a Rambo film.

For a good while, the third option was my first choice. It was dark now and I could clearly see the flickering lights of town just below me. All I had to do was jump.

Instead, and very much out of character, I *reasoned* that the second option was a better bet. So, like Napoleon leaving Moscow, I slowly and painfully clawed my way back.

I staggered into town well after sunrise. At the same café from the day before, I saw my would-be Dutch friends enjoying a late breakfast. "Folwell," they exclaimed, you look like you had a rougher night than us?!"

"Probably so," I said.

"We missed you at Happy Hour. How was your walk in the woods above Lake Atitlán?"

"Memorable," I said. "So much so, I may have to write it down."

Twenty-one years later—just enough time to recover from the ordeal—I finally did.

Leaving the Compound
And Finding One Love
(the Hard Way) in Jamaica

I should never listen to Todd.

When I told my friend Todd, aka Choupique (shoo-pick), we were going to Jamaica, he lit up like a sparkler on the Fourth of July. "Dude!" he said, "Ya gotta go to Fonthill Nature Reserve! They got crocodiles that chase iguanas up frickin trees. They're practically arboreal!"

"Hmmm," I said. "Maybe so…"

Note: I later discovered that Todd had never actually been to the reserve. Nor Jamaica for that matter! His recommendation was based on an article he had stumbled across in some obscure biology journal. Always check your sources!

Most Americans who travel to Jamaica stay on a compound. They go to an all-inclusive resort like Sandals or Hedonism VIII, drink margaritas by the pool and swim with dolphins in a fenced-in lagoon. They take a Carnival cruise without ever leaving port.

My wife and I had a different idea. We wanted to experience *the real* Jamaica. We were gonna discover the next generation of Wailers in Trench Town, take a pilgrimage to Nine Mile, the birthplace of Bob Marley, drink Blue Mountain coffee IN the Blue Mountains, find literary in-

Peter Tosh Park in Jamaica (something from the field)

spiration at Ian Fleming's *Goldeneye* and Noël Coward's *Firefly*, call on the elusive doctor bird in Marshall's Pen, "worship" with Rastafarians, dine on jerk, and run, up-right, with Usain Bolt! Unbeknownst to my wife, I was also motivated by the popular 1972 poster of Sintra Bronte emerging from the water wearing nothing but a tee shirt. Who wouldn't want to "come to Jamaica and feel alright!?"

Our plan was to fly into Kingston armed with an old copy of *Lonely Planet*, rent a car, tool around the island for two weeks without reservations, recover for a few days on the rocks above Negril, and then return home via Mon-tego Bay. We would get as far off the compound as humanly possible.

My dad likes to say, "A bad plan is better than no plan at all." Unfortunately for us, our "bad plan" was, well, no plan at all!

———

If Milton needed inspiration for *Paradise Lost*, he could have easily found it in the Caribbean. Jamaica is, without a doubt, one of the most beautiful places on the planet! But, as a therapist might say, "It has issues."

On the other side of the resort walls, the former British colony is dirt poor. Its infrastructure is crumbling and order is hard to come by. Entire swaths of the island seem to be teetering on the edge of anarchy! At one point, we stayed at a big house deep in the jungle. It resembled the plantation in *Apocalypse Now Redux*. The expats who ran the place were desperately clinging to a bygone era! They served Beef Wellington and high tea as the world around them slowly collapsed.

The roads in Jamaica are terrible and the drivers are even worse. "Jammin' in the name of the Lord" (I hope you like jammin' too?), locals race around the island on the "wrong" side of the street at breakneck speeds. They're the only thing in the country that moves fast. All along the highways there were signs that read, "Don't let your overtake be your undertake!" and "Don't be in a rush to get to eternity!" Obviously, they were part of a failed safety campaign.

Over the trail rated course of two weeks, we survived numerous near collisions, several flat tires, a flash flood, an all-night reggae rap rave, food poisoning from undercooked Juici Patties, and an almost endless barrage of

With a souvenir from Jamaica,
the famous poster of Sintra Bronte (2011)

panhandlers who always enquired, "Can I get ya somethin from the field man?"

Limping our way toward Negril, between the Black River and White House on the southern coast, we passed an inconspicuous sign that read, "Fonthill Nature Reserve." Before I could ask, my wife just shook her head. "No!"

"But Choupique said they have arboreal crocodiles," I pleaded.

"We're going to Negril," she said.

"But Todd lit up like a sparkler," I said. "He'd be seriously disappointed if we missed it."

Always the pragmatist, my wife pointed out, "We don't have water, a map, or a phone. And, it's getting late!"

"We'll only stop for a second," I persisted. "We'll pop in, look for crocodiles in the trees, and then leave. We'll stay for a half an hour at most."

"At most!" she said.

Pulling in to the parking lot, we were surprised to find a huge crowd. It was Sunday, and the locals were having a party on the beach. They were listening to music, cooking jerk, drinking, smoking, and dancing; no one was looking for crocodiles.

The park had no welcome center, ranger, brochure or trailhead. To enter the reserve, we had to limbo our way under a rickety barbed wire fence. The revelers looked at us as though we were crazy. "Why would you go there when you could be here?" they thought.

They had a point.

With mangroves on the left and ocean on the right, we walked along the beach until we could no longer hear the music. And, it was beautiful. We came across a secluded bay with sugar white sand and crystal clear water. Nurse sharks were mating in the shallows and dolphins were hunting beyond the reef. It looked like the blue lagoon in *Blue Lagoon*.

"Maybe Todd was right?" I thought.

We took a swim and relaxed on the beach. Then, I made a fateful suggestion: "Let's take the mangroves back. Maybe we'll see one of those cool crocodiles?"

My wife objected, but again, I was persistent. "Todd would surely be disappointed."

So, we took a spindly trail that led in the general direction of the park entrance. In retrospect, I don't think it was a trail at all, but rather a path frequented by foolish

American Crocodile in
Jamaica

pigs. We walked and
walked and walked
until we came to a
dead end, and then
another, and another
and another. At about
the time I realized we
were seriously lost, I
also realized that my
wife was about to have her "vacation meltdown." These
"episodes" occur at least once a trip, usually prompt-
ed by a decision of mine based on a recommendation
from Todd. With my palms facing the ground I pleaded,
"Please, please don't have a meltdown!"

Before I could say more, my wife, wearing flip flops,
stepped in a massive pile of crocodile crap. As she
screamed, the beast that had most likely created the mess,
bounded toward us. It was as big as the biggest alligator I
had ever seen, but much uglier. It had a pointy snout and
huge teeth that obviously didn't fit in its mouth. I thought
about climbing a tree, but quickly remembered, "They're
&%$! arboreal!" Just before the animal tore us into hu-
man ceviche, it unexpectedly (and thankfully) turned and
plunged into the swamp. Unlike us, it actually knew where
it was.

For the next ten minutes my wife hurled expletives (de-
servedly so) at me, Choupique, *Lonely Planet*, Jamaica, the
nature reserve, and its unique endemic flora and fauna.

When she finally tuckered out, I heard, off in the distance, the unmistakable, albeit faint sound of Gregory Isaacs singing about a night nurse, a protagonist we would desperately need later that evening. "All we have to do is follow the music," I said. "It'll be as easy as Hansel and Gretel picking up bread crumbs in the forest."

It wasn't. Instead, it was more like laying siege to a medieval castle, dodging boiling oil, arrows, and insults: "Your mother was a hamster and your father smelt of elderberries!"

Using a beach towel as a shield, we plowed our way through a gauntlet of sludge, stickers, fire ants, and deer flies. For about forty-five minutes, we bushwhacked our way toward Peter Tosh, Jimmy Cliff, and Burning Spear— in silence. We forged our own trail of tears.

Covered in blood, sweat, and welts, we finally arrived at the rickety barbed wire fence. On the other side, the reggae jam was still going strong. The crowd again stared at us in disbelief. "What is wrong with these white people?" they thought. Then, an old man wearing nothing but torn jeans and long dreadlocks walked up to us, handed me a Red Stripe and asked, "Can I get ya somethin from the field man?"

"Yes," I said. "By all means!"

One love!

Epilogue

Throughout our vacation/ordeal, I kept telling my wife, "Wherever ya go, you gotta live off the land. You should always eat what ya see!" Since we saw nothing but chickens and goats all over the island, I suggested we eat, well, chicken and goat. My wife approved of the former, but frowned on the latter. I, unfortunately, partook of both.

I spent the first five days back in New Orleans at Touro Hospital with acute abdominal pain. The GI doctor bleated, "You probably ate 'baaaaaaaad' goat."

Author's note: Crocodile crap and ruminant digestive troubles aside, my wife and I love Jamaica. The island is beautiful and the people are wonderful. Whenever we go back, we always leave the compound, eat chicken, and ignore recommendations from my dear friend Choupique.

Note 2: For a primer on the grittier side of Jamaica, see the 1972 film, *The Harder They Come*. The soundtrack is arguably the best reggae album of all time.

Bad Brakes in Colima*
A Test of the Marriage on the Volcano of Fire

My good friend Todd, aka Choupique, is a biologist and birder. Whenever he travels, he consults the *Sibley Guide to Birds* and *National Geographic Expeditions*. My wife and I on the other hand use the UNESCO World Heritage List and *Condé Nast*.

When I told Choupique we were going to Guadalajara and the Pacific Coast of Mexico, his eyes bulged from his head like a great horned owl on a moonless night. "DUDE," he said, "ya gotta go to Parque Nacional Nevado de Colima! It's on my bucket list. They've got chestnut-sided shrike-vireos, cinnamon-bellied flowerpiercers, and buff-breasted flycatchers. You might even see an Aztec thrush or a great swallow-tailed swift!"

Having taken Todd's advice before on a disastrous trip to Jamaica, I politely smiled, shook my head in agreement and then, privately, dismissed his suggestion unequivocally.

After exploring the colonial riches of Mexico's second largest city, my wife and I rented an old Volkswagen Beetle, which, at the time, was still being made at a plant in

---

* On just about every trip, my wife and I experience some kind of calamity, usually caused by a decision of mine. She refers to it as "a test of the marriage." Colima was an exam!

My wife with our bug in Mexico

Puebla. I had learned to drive in a VW, so when I saw the bug, I lit up like a firefly.

On the winding road to the Pacific Coast, we passed a sign for Colima. "Don't even go there," my wife warned.

"But, according to *Let's Go Mexico*," I said, "Colima is a quaint colonial town well worth visiting.'"**

"After three days in Guadala-HORROR," my wife said (she obviously wasn't nearly as impressed with the city's colonial riches), "I'm ready for a little beach-side R&R."

"Let's just stay the night," I insisted. "It'll be an adventure."

Like Lee with Longstreet before Gettysburg, my misguided persistence eventually paid off. We turned around and headed straight for "a test of the marriage."

** My wife and I would later refer to the guidebook as, "Let's Go to Hell!"

That evening, in the *somewhat* quaint town of Colima, I asked locals about the nearby volcano.

"*El Volcán de Fuego es muy bonito*," they said. "The Volcano of Fire is very beautiful. And, it's only two hours away."

"Hmmmmm," I thought.

"NO!" my wife countered, obviously having read my ill-conceived thought.

"But it's on Choupique's bucket list," I persisted.

"HIS bucket list," she clarified. "Don't forget, Todd almost got us killed in Jamaica!"

"Let's give him another shot," I pleaded. "Besides, it's only two hours away."

Once again, like Robert E. Lee, this time with General George Pickett before his ill-fated, up-hill charge, I somehow rallied my beleaguered and incredulous troop(s).

After a two-hour drive in the opposite direction of the beach, we arrived at the entrance of Parque Nacional Nevado de Colima. Looking up at a map of the park, my wife just grimaced. I cursed Todd beneath my breath and then tried to do the math. (I was a humanities major.) There was a winding road to the top marked out in kilometers. I figured the round-trip would take us no more than an hour. Obviously, I underestimated the length of a kilometer, and I overestimated the power (and health) of our vehicle. We would spend the rest of the day (and almost the rest of our lives) on that godforsaken mountain.

Having come so far, I was now determined to summit Fuego; having come so far, my wife was now determined to see me fail. So, in a simmering stew of contempt, we slowly climbed the face of Colima—in silence. The test of the marriage on the Volcano of Fire had commenced!

An hour into the climb and less than halfway to the crater, we passed a ranger station. Men sitting next to all-terrain vehicles stared at our vintage bug in disbelief. "¡*Que idiotas!*" they thought (and most likely said).

Just below the snow-covered peak, we came around a turn and discovered that there had been a landslide. I hopped out to figure a way around it. At that moment, after more than two hours of smoldering silence, my wife, like a volcano, finally blew her top! She spewed out an endless flow of molten expletives, culminating in a simple demand: "Get me off this &%$@ing! mountain!"

Lee was now negotiating terms of surrender at Appomattox.

As I painstakingly turned the bug around on the sliver of road, my wife pulled out *Let's Go* and flipped to the section on Puerto Vallarta, a beautiful city on the coast with a name even the locals can't pronounce.***

Being a flatlander from Louisiana, I wasn't accustomed to driving down a mountain. I figured the steep decline would bring us to the bottom (and eventually the beach) lickety-split. Sure enough, within seconds, we were barreling down the Volcano of Fire.

When I pressed on the brakes to slow us down though, there was nothing. Stomping on the pedal as if it were a roach, there was still NOTHING. I turned to my wife and calmly said, "Houston, we have a problem." She looked at me with daggers in her eyes, dropped the book, and fired off another bevvy of expletives.

Then, I had a revelation. I remembered the 1972 "Su-

*** Just outside Puerto Vallarta, we experienced yet another test of the marriage in "The Palapa In Yelapa."

per" Beetle I'd had in college. Friends and I would take it on a country road. At about thirty miles an hour, I'd pop the clutch, pull the emergency brake and spin the wheel. It was a lot of fun and only slightly dangerous. I figured I could do the same thing here, without spinning the wheel of course. I'd stop the Bug, save us, and (possibly) the marriage!

When I pulled up on the emergency brake though, to my horror, I discovered it wasn't even attached. I held it out to my wife like a dropped relay baton. My wife screamed and then opened the door; she was ready to jump!

In desperation, I threw the bug into first gear. All four puny cylinders shrieked in protest like an angry shrew; but the German car, "*hecho en Mexico*," refused to slow down. Pulled by gravity over loose gravel, we were completely out of control.

On one side there was a sheer cliff that dropped off hundreds of feet (and probably thousands of kilometers!); on the other side, there was the "beautiful" El Volcán de Fuego. After barely maneuvering a hairpin switchback, and knowing I couldn't possibly do it again, I decided to throw the car into the side of the mountain. Hopefully, we would survive the impact, and the rental car insurance policy would cover the damage.****

Fortunately for us, nature, physics, and luck intervened. There was a shallow gully on the edge of the road that had been carved out by years of erosion. It was filled to the brim with powder-like pumice. The left side tires

---

**** At a motel in Manzanilla, we finally read the fine print in the rental car's insurance policy. Apparently, there was no coverage on unpaved roads. Imagine that?

plowed into the dust, which brought the car to a gradual, harmless stop.

Stuck on the side of the mountain with our Volkswagen Beetle with bad brakes, I then made yet another marriage-testing mistake. I pulled out John Barry's book, *Rising Tide* about the great Mississippi River flood of 1927 and plopped down on the back seat to read. It was cold outside, and besides, I figured someone would eventually spot our fire engine red bug.

Like the Greenland ice sheet under a thick cloud of greenhouse gases, my wife, again, began to melt down. Expletives fell like ash from Mount St. Helens. She grabbed a jacket and a bottle of water and started marching defiantly down the mountain. I sheepishly followed.

Every few minutes, we would scream over the edge, "*¡Ayúdanos!* Help us!"

Like Albert Finney in *Under the Volcano*, I longed for a stiff shot of mescaline.

After about forty-five minutes, a park ranger on an ATV came to our rescue. Ironically, his name was Angel, but we ended up calling him *Nuestro Salvador de Colima*, Our Savior from Colima.

After confirming that our brakes were indeed shot, he offered to drive us down in our own car. Like Lee before Chancellorsville, he convinced us that it could be done. He also told us with some authority that just about every year a foreigner died on the mountain. "We were betting," he said, "you two would be the next."

My wife sat in the front with the door ajar; I sat in the back, clinging to a frayed seatbelt and a prayer.

Relying solely on the clutch, Angel drove us down the

mountain. Like teenagers on a rollercoaster, my wife and I screamed the entire way down.

When we finally reached the bottom, we kissed the ground and hugged Angel, *Nuestro Salvador de Colima*. We gave him twenty dollars, a bottle of Kahlúa, and an open invitation to visit us on flat ground in New Orleans.

In Manzanilla, we switched out our Bug, cursed Choupique one more time for good measure, and then headed for the beach. The test was over—for now.

The Palapa in Yelapa
Where there has Never
Been Such a Night!

The Night of the Iguana by Tennessee Williams takes place in a rundown hotel just outside of Puerto Vallarta, Mexico. In the trailer for the 1964 film adaptation, the narrator says, "Since man has known woman, there has never been such a night."

More than thirty years later, my wife and I stayed at a hotel in Yelapa, a small town just south of Puerto Vallarta. As long as I've known my wife, there has never been such a night!

———

My wife and I had just barely survived a harrowing trek up (and down) the Volcano of Fire in Colima. Our wits and marriage had been driven (literally) to the edge. We were in dire need of a sun-drenched beach and an IV dripping with tequila. Fortunately for us, Puerto Vallarta had both.

In this beautiful seaside city, we swam in a tranquil turquoise bay, walked a long crescent beach, ate fresh ceviche on the docks, and drank frozen margaritas beneath swaying palms. We also took a number of short excursions up and down the coast with expats from cold climates. On one, we visited *The Night of the Iguana* hotel where, suppos-

Yelapa, Mexico

edly, "there has never been such a night."

Exploring the city, we noticed flyers and posters promoting a "romantic" hotel in the nearby village of Yelapa. Like AOL in the 80s (or Rosetta Stone today), the ads were everywhere. A somewhat seasoned traveler, I was leery. So, I asked locals about Yelapa. They all said the same thing: "*Vale la pena por el dia no mas*. It's a worthwhile day trip."

Then, like an irrational character from a Tennessee Williams play (Is there any other kind?), I ignored their advice and my own apprehension. I asked my wife, "Why don't we go and stay the night? It'll be romantic."

"Absolutely not," she thundered! "It's romantic here. And, our hotel has AC!"

"But it'll be an adventure," I insisted.

"We already HAD an adventure in Colima," she said.

"We almost died, remember?!"

"But this would be like a second honeymoon," I continued—and continued and continued until I finally wore down her far better judgment.

The next day, we jumped on a boat with a gaggle of day-trippers and headed for Yelapa.

Located on a picturesque bay only accessible by water, Yelapa is like a Latin American version of a town on the Cinque Terre in Italy. Perched on the rocks above the Pacific Ocean and surrounded by dense jungle, it was practically designed for a postcard. "THIS would be my vindication for Colima," I thought.

In Yelapa, my wife and I rode horses into the surrounding hills, snorkeled along a nearby reef and ate barbecued shrimp on the beach. It was a perfect day.

In the afternoon, all of the tourists (and most of the locals) packed up, jumped in boats, and headed back to Puerto Vallarta. Within minutes, Yelapa was a ghost town.

This time my wife was leery. Sensing her concern and always the optimist, I said, "Looks like we'll have paradise all to ourselves!"

After a beautiful sunset, the town's sole generator fired up. It coughed violently as the lights flickered. Then, after about an hour, the machine suddenly expired. The little town of Yelapa was shrouded in darkness. It was only eight o'clock.

My wife and I sat at a table on the beach. I lit a candle and opened a bottle of wine. "Now THIS is romantic," I said.

"We'll see," my wife replied as she swatted a mosquito.

Then, like Braddock's expedition in the French and

Indian War, we were ambushed. Swarms of flying insects with evil intentions attacked from all sides. Like Jessica Tandy in *The Birds*, we fled in horror to the shelter of our palapa, a small primitive bungalow made of bamboo and thatch.

There, my wife and I huddled beneath a thin shield of mosquito netting hanging over the bed. The netting, like a used coffee filter, was soon clogged with determined insects.

Inside the greenhouse of netting and thatch, the palapa was a veritable oven. There was no "cool ocean breeze" as advertised in the flyers. Within minutes, we were swimming in our own sweat.

Trying to bring a little levity to the situation, my wife jokingly referenced a popular ad at the time, saying, "You know, we could have stayed at a Motel 6. They actually have a light, and they leave it on for you!"

I invoked Shakespeare exclaiming, "AC, AC, my kingdom for AC!"

Then I pointed out that the incessant buzz created by the mosquitos was like white noise. "Perhaps it will help us sleep?" I said.

"I doubt it," my wife replied. "It sounds like we have OTHER roommates!"

Like Carl Sagan staring into the cosmos, we looked up and saw billions and billions of glowing eyes looking back at us. The owners of those eyes squeaked, chirped, hissed, howled, shrieked, wailed, and croaked. It was a veritable cacophony.

Some of our guests were probably in love. The Casanovas were simply calling out to potential mates. Others, obviously vegetarians, were devouring the thatch. We heard scratching and crunching, as shards of palmetto fronds fell from the ceiling like confetti. The rest though were definitely carnivores; and they saw us as a cheap and convenient Fogo de Chão.

During the middle of the siege, my wife made a break for the bathroom. Halfway there, she stepped in a huge pile of warm poo that had obviously been deposited by one of our nocturnal visitors. She screamed so loud, the police in Puerto Vallarta were put on edge. Then, she stepped on the visitor, a massive, fat and not so happy marine toad. My wife screamed again as the toad lunged for the toilet.

Back beneath the netting, my wife finally began to melt down. She had had enough! She scolded me, Yelapa, Mexico, and NAFTA. She even cursed James Taylor for singing, "It sounds so simple, I just have to go."

As the expletives flew, a bug bit me on the butt. Then others stung me on the neck, arm and foot. Like the Turks at the gates of Constantinople in 1453, the mosquitos had finally forced their way in! It was a bloodbath.

As my wife and I flailed beneath the breached netting, not in passion but in pain, we heard a loud thunderclap. "Perhaps rain would drive away the bugs and cool down the palapa," we thought.

It was wishful thinking.

The vegetarians that were eating the thatch had successfully bored holes in the roof. Our ceiling was a sieve. Inside the palapa, rain came down like, well, rain. The insects, now angered by the deluge, bit us out of spite.

At about four in the morning, my wife and I finally abandoned our embattled palapa. For the next three hours, we sat on the beach waiting for the first boat out, swatting sandflies and, desperate for sleep, counting waves like sheep.

As the sun slowly climbed over the critter-infested jungle, a small boat filled with eager and excited tourists appeared on the horizon. Covered in sweat and welts, and looking more forlorn than Tom Hanks in *Cast Away*, WE were their welcoming committee. Seeing us, they pulled out their flyers and reviewed them with trepidation. We waded into the surf and climbed aboard before the boat had even landed.

Like Texans after the Alamo, we would always remember the Palapa in Yelapa. "There has never been such a night!"

A Midlife Crisis
In a 1968 Land Rover Series IIA

A friend of mine claims there's no such thing as a mid-life crisis. Having survived more than a dozen, I beg to differ.

My fourth, like the Fourth Crusade, was one of the most memorable.

It started out like all the rest. I quit my job and my wife freaked out. I reread *Siddhartha* by Hermann Hesse and *On the Road* by Jack Kerouac. I watched *The Motorcycle Diaries*, the story about Che Guevara's inspirational trek across South America. I contemplated living in a cabin on a pond like Henry David Thoreau or buying a farm in Oaxaca to raise agave (for mescal of course), avocados, pistachios, and goats.

In my quest for direction, I also surfed the web. At one point, late at night and after several glasses of wine, I ended up on Ebay in the Motors section.

Note: Most guys of a certain age covet cars like Corvettes, Porsches, and Camaros. Not me. I have an affinity for 1960s vintage British vehicles. I like Sunbeams, Spitfires, and MGs. But, my all-time favorite is the Land Rover. The Landy, as it's known to aficionados, was the British answer to the American Jeep. Featured in films like *The Gods Must Be Crazy* and *Ace Ventura: When Nature Calls*, it's

Driving my 1968 Land Rover back from Georgia, 2007

become emblematic of the African safari.* The car could be taken apart and put back together (while driving) with only a screwdriver and a pair of pliers. It was made out of aluminum, its roof could be used as a boat, and it could be started with a crank like a Model T. It was the epitome of utilitarian simplicity. There were no frilly bells and whistles like power steering or seatbelts.

Back on Ebay, bored and in need of a "cheap" thrill, I placed a bid on a cute forty-year-old Series IIA, knowing it would quickly be overturned. I shut down the browser and went to sleep.

The next morning, I found my wife sobbing in front

---

* Scores of Land Rovers were destroyed in the Jim Carrey film. Even though it was a comedy, I wept like a child.

of the computer screen. She was staring at a message that read, "Congratulations! You are the proud owner of a 1968 Land Rover!"

My midlife crisis had become our latest "test of the marriage!"

To make matters worse, the car I needed like another hole in the head was in Georgia, about an hour and a half outside of Atlanta. I had to pick it up. My good friend, Graham Gibby, always up for an adventure, generously agreed to drive me there and follow me back. (It's been years, but I'm still repaying the favor!)

When we arrived and saw the diminutive Tonka Toy-like vehicle, we immediately dubbed it, "The Hobbit."

"I got good news and bad news," said the owner. "The good news is I'm throwin' in a custom-made rack. The bad news is the radio I installed just stopped workin'."

"Thanks, and no problem," I said. "More importantly, do you think it can make it to New Orleans?"

He hesitated and then said, "Probably." Sizing me up, he added, "Not sure about you though."

I didn't think much about the *previous* owner's good and bad news until I got on the road. The tall metal rack rattled like a huge steal maraca; and there was no other "music" to drown out the noise. As in the mockumentary, *This is Spinal Tap*, the decibel level in the cab was a deafening 11!

Speaking of spines, The Hobbit's short wheelbase and lack of suspension had chiropractors drooling. Over the accelerated course of my crisis, I slipped a disk, pinched a nerve, and cracked my tailbone.

The next thing I noticed on the road was the heat. It

The "Hobbit" parked in front of my house, 2007

was July, and my Flintstone car had no AC. (Note: Having been designed in Solihull, England, it did have a killer heater though.) Inside the aluminum shell, it was a glass-blowing furnace.

While the British may have built an empire "on which the sun never sets," they were less adept at making car windows. Instead of rolling up and down, the Rover's slid from side to side, only opening halfway. As I drove, a thin shaft of warm air blew gently across the back of my neck —while the rest of my body burned in eternal hellfire.

Whenever I stopped at a light for more than a minute, I'd spontaneously combust. Fortunately, I was able to douse the flames with my own sweat!

Every two hours, I'd pull off to the side of the road and

collapse in the aptly titled emergency lane.

The Landy drove like a tractor.** And, it wasn't exactly a speedster. Going downhill with a tailwind, it topped out at about fifty miles an hour. Cars that passed me on the Interstate, basically every car (and a few bicycles), honked in appreciation for the silly car and its brave (and foolish) driver.

Somewhere around Montgomery, Alabama, The Hobbit started hemorrhaging oil like BP. Fortunately, Gibby and I were able to fix it with only a screwdriver and a pair of pliers.

The eight-hour trip took us fourteen. When we finally arrived in New Orleans and my wife saw our "new" car up close, she cried again.

In many ways The Hobbit was ideal for the Trail Rated® roads of New Orleans. It could ford a pothole like a Higgins landing craft, and it could fit into the tightest French Quarter parking space. Its aluminum chassis was rustproof; and, it almost goes without saying, having a roof that doubles as a boat is lagniappe for the bayous, canals, and streets of the Crescent City.

To pay for the midlife crisis, I got a new job working with schools. When I'd pull up in The Hobbit, kids would run out screaming as though I were the Good Humor Man. Then, when they saw me, defeated, sweaty and humorless, they'd run back to class—screaming.

My wife once tried to drive The Hobbit. After fighting with the gears for three rounds, she gave up. She never got behind the wheel again.

A friend of mine who is a doctor in North Carolina

** Modeled after a tractor, the first Land Rover in 1948 had a steering wheel in the middle.

came down to visit. I took him for a spin in my Amish car. When we got back, a bit frazzled, he turned to me and said, "That thing's a deathtrap! It (or your wife) is gonna kill ya!"

The next day I put it back on Ebay—for somebody else's midlife crisis!

Epilogue

Over the years, The Hobbit has changed hands a number of times. Undoubtedly, it was purchased by men in the midst of a midlife crisis. Its current owner calls it "The Mule."

For my next midlife crisis, which, by the way, started about a half an hour ago, I'm gonna take a millennial approach. I'll buy an electric bicycle, study circus arts, and grow a beard.

My Educational Philosophy
In Reams and Reams of Jargon

As a middle schooler might confess, "I am a loser." I now have a huge scarlet "L" watermarked on my resume and another PowerPointed against my forehead. You see, I recently applied for a number of school positions, but was soundly and brutally rebuffed each and every time. After receiving the umpteenth *thin* envelope, I actually composed my own sad theme song. It went something like this:

Rejection Jection, what's your defection? Hooking up mirrors and checking your reflection. Rejection Jection, how's that complexion? It could be your smile or maybe your inflexion? There has to be something that's bringing you dejection… (with apologies to *Schoolhouse Rock*)

Bottom line, I felt like Lee Majors splayed out on the cold black tarmac. Unfortunately, in my case, the Bionics department was plumb out of cash, and Farrah Fawcett had already moved on. Even though I'm a gentile, I felt verklempt.

So, like a trooper (or a narcissistic twit), I sat down and compiled a list of possible, though not all that plausible, explanations. I then whittled them down to the most esoteric—the ones that displaced as much blame as possible and that could be remedied with the least amount of discomfort. I finally convinced myself that it was my answer to the oh-so *pivotal* educational philosophy question that had stymied my career aspirations (and not being fired on the cover of a major newspaper). All I had to do was trim it down and shore it up. Avoid unnecessary tangents (In an interview once, I ended up blathering on about Tanzania and the historical significance of the yoke.) and flaunt my pedagogical dexterity. I would say it all in five minutes or less. Presto! The job would be mine.

"So, Mr. Dunbar, what is your educational philosophy?"

Hmmm. What an intriguing question. Off the top of my head:

I believe that all kids can learn. That knowledge is power, that diversity is a strength, that less is more, and that yes, technology is just a tool. I believe in academic choice, digital literacy, block scheduling, sustained silent reading, the writing process, project-based learning, standardized grading, interdisciplinary and differentiated instruction, constructivism, manipulatives, journals, portfolios, and rubrics.

I believe that we have a responsibility to make accommodations for learning differences (auditory, kinesthetic, visual, etc.) and that we must recognize and address multiple intelligences. In my humble opinion, all education should be special.

I believe that teaching is not a vocation, but rather a calling. That we are change agents, facilitators, mentors, and coaches—guides on the sides and not sages on stages.

When it comes to schools and classrooms, our students deserve a rich and stimulating, risk-free, equitable learning environment. I believe that education should be child-centered, real world, and hands-on. We must always be on the lookout for the latest and greatest, tried and true, research-based "best practices." We must stay on-task, teach from bell to bell, meet or surpass academic benchmarks, leverage all available resources, and cultivate a culture of high achievement.

When it comes to literacy, I prefer a balanced approach. While phonics can certainly be fun, we must always consider the big picture and the whole child. Echo, choral, and guided reading can all be enlisted to accelerate English language development. Our young authors should be given an opportunity to read and write all the way across the curriculum.

I also think that we should focus on higher-order, critical thinking skills. Old school, rote memorization is still important, but today, in the global economy and in a multicultural world, metacognition is much more relevant. We can no longer rely on obsolete (and dull) worksheets, basal readers, direct instruction, and pacing charts. Skill and drill is well deserving of its alternative moniker: "drill and kill." Instead, we should ask tough, open-ended questions that challenge and motivate our students—that spark their curiosity and that ignite their creativity. We must go well beyond a mile wide and an inch deep!

*We should use alternative, varied, and authentic assessments that are both reliable and valid. Then, we must triangulate the results from these formative and summative measures, criterion and norm-referenced tests, formal and informal observations, peer and self-evaluations, etc. and use them to make wise, data-driven decisions—to identify strengths and challenges, to refine and align the curriculum, and, most importantly, to meet and even exceed individual and group learner' needs. Keep in mind, we should never teach to the test, but rather to the standards **and** the child.*

I like Bloom, Dewey, Wiggins, Marzano, Stiggins, McTighe, Jacobs, Holmes, Stigler, Darling-Hammond, and, with a few grains of salt, Kohn.

To make AYP, we must draft an SIP that is a living, breathing document. Of course, the key is to work smarter, not harder. Scaffold-

ing and transparency are essential.

We must also design, build, and support true professional learning communities where collaboration and cooperation are the norm and not the exception. From site-based management and whole-faculty study groups to distance learning and lesson study, any and all initiatives must be accompanied by adequate, meaningful, appropriate, and ongoing professional development—PD in which there is significant faculty buy-in or, better yet, ownership.

As educators, we must be proactive, passionate, innovative, visionary, interactive, critical, impactful, dynamic, collegial, strategic, holistic, synergistic, and kidcentric.

*Unfortunately, we live in a nation at risk. It's time for a new paradigm. We must do everything in our power to close the achievement gap and bridge the digital divide. We must initiate comprehensive, whole-school reform—raise the bar and share accountability. To this end, parental involvement is absolutely critical. **All** stakeholders need to be active participants in this vital process. We must guarantee that not a single child is ever left behind!*

In an increasingly flat world, we must make good schools great, adopt a FISH philosophy, understand by design, beat the bell curve, and figure out who the hell moved that stinky cheese.

Our ultimate goal must be to create a community of lifelong learners.

*You know, children **are** our future!*

Yep, that's about it. Oh, I almost forgot, all you really need to know, you probably already learned in kindergarten.

Note: I didn't get the job.

My Resume 2.0

After "The Bribe" and countless rejections, I figured I needed to reinvent myself. I asked a former colleague of mine to help me create a new resume. She said traditional resumes had become obsolete. She said that even LinkedIn profiles were now passé. She suggested that I tell prospective employers about the real me, about the person beyond academic degrees, job experiences, and recognized accomplishments like being fired on the cover of a major newspaper. She said I needed to point out the small, ordinary things that set me apart. So, here's what I came up with:

- I have over four hundred friends on Facebook! And, I actually know many of them.

- I listen to NPR—a lot. I named my pet salamander Terry Gross; whenever I mention Accra, the capital of Ghana, I try to say it like Ofeibea Quist-Arcton; and I always follow the advice of The Writer's Almanac: "Be well, do good work and keep in touch."

- According to my fitness tracker, I sometimes exceed my workout goals!

- I possess at least three of *The 7 Habits of Highly Effective People*.

- Even though I have cable, I often watch **PBS**. (OK, my wife and I sometimes watch *Downton Abbey*.)

- I have a Subscription to *Mental Floss*.

- Most of the time I choose paper over plastic.

- I can often be found working in coffee shops.

- My LinkedIn profile was "viewed" eight times in just one week!

- I use Apple products.

- I can follow at least 48 percent of what Fareed Zakaria is talking about.

- I once posted an update to Facebook that got nearly forty "likes"!

- I submit letters to the editor. Some get published. Mostly online.

- I won Josh Groban tickets for being caller number four.

- To save water, I sometimes pee outside. (Note: It also sets a good example for my dog Mole, pronounced like the Mexican sauce and not the rodent.)

- I have a library card.

- Millennials say I'm very "intentional."

- I know other documentary filmmakers besides Ken Burns.

- I once owned property in Atlantic City.[*]

---

[*] While playing Monopoly.

- I fell off the world's highest active volcano, Cotopaxi, and lived to tell about it.

- I recently saved a bunch of money on my car insurance by switching to Geico.

- I write limericks.

- People tell me that my impression of a cat coughing up a hairball is spot on.

- I received a "Certificate of Completion" for reading Jon Stewart's book, *America*. I am now "fully qualified to practice, participate in or found a democracy."

- I know a lot of trivia, especially about animals and geography.

- I actually read *Finnegan's Wake* and *The Power and the Glory*. OK, I read several pages and then got the CliffsNotes. OK, even after reading the CliffsNotes, I had no idea what they were about. OK, maybe I should remove this one from my resume?

- I rarely confuse then and than, further and farther, or there, their, and they're.

- I once felt my phone vibrating in my pocket even though it wasn't there.

- I have endorsements on LinkedIn for pirogue paddling, cuy (guinea pig) husbandry, and Dutch oven cooking.

- I have a man bun. OK, it may just be a cowlick, but it's a man bun to me!

- At a bar in Durham, North Carolina, I've had the high score in Galaga for over twenty years!

- I'm considering going back to vinyl.

- I get mostly favorable reviews when I stay in Airbnb's.

- I have my own hashtag.

- I adopted a goat and three chickens from Heifer International.

- In that online test to determine whether or not you are a robot, I almost always pass.

- I sometimes watch films that were originally screened at Sundance and Cannes. One time I even watched a foreign film that had subtitles!

- I eat kale.

- Though I've never won, I often compete in the *New Yorker's* Caption Contest.**

- I only login to ESPN in the workplace during the Saints' season, Grand Slam tennis events, PTI, MMA title bouts, and all major badminton tournaments.

- I am a longstanding member of the prestigious Hair Club for Men.

- i sometimes write using all lower-case letters.

- I have a really high Sleep Number.

- I may have invented the sport of extreme downhill unicycling. Seriously.

- I hang out in neighborhoods that haven't yet been discovered.

- I aspire to live in a tiny house.

** I think it's rigged!

- Except for similes, I, you know, rarely use the term, "like."

- According to Duolingo, I'm 17 percent fluent in Esperanto!

- I once castrated a sheep with my teeth. True story. No, I'm not proud.***

- I fall well. But, I almost always get back up!

*** Strangely, he didn't seem to mind.

My Favorite Artist

Yes, I know I'm a bit biased, but my dad is definitely my favorite artist.

This wasn't always the case. When I was a kid, I thought his work was just plain weird. He "painted" with string, envelopes, metal leaf, egg emulsion, and rabbit-skin glue. He used augers, belt sanders, and even birdshot to "mine the surface" of his sculptures. He tore strips of cloth and dropped them haphazardly from a second-floor balcony, waiting for what he called "an accidental triumph" to occur. He drew inspiration from colonial santos, marsh grass, and old plaster walls in the French Quarter. He admired the work of Cézanne, Rothko, Modigliani, Franz Kline, Willem de Kooning, and others who made weird art.

His work looked like stuff, well, I could do. But, of course, it didn't and I couldn't.

When I was in high school, I took a few drawing classes. One evening while doing homework, my father asked if he could help. "No," I said, "you wouldn't understand. We're studying the human anatomy; your work is all abstract."

He took out a pencil and quickly sketched a figure that could have easily passed for the work of a Renaissance master. "Of course, I can capture reality son," he said. "I just choose not to. I'm after something different."

249

My dad surfing, ca. 1975

My dad also hung out
with weird people. There
was Enrique Alférez, Bob
Helmer, Shearly Grode,
Lynn Emery, Jean Se-
idenberg, Ida Kohlmeyer,
and George Dureau. They
would come over to our
weird house and discuss
weird topics, things like the
evolution of action painting post Jackson Pollock, the in-
fluence of Mexican and Southern regionalism on the new
abstract expressionism, the relevance of Pop Art and War-
hol's "Factory," and the shifting nucleus of the art world in
New York City. I had no idea what they were talking about.

In 2006, there was an exhibit at the Newcomb Gallery
called *Capturing Southern Bohemia*. It featured images from
New Orleans in the 1950s taken by the famous fashion
photographer, Jack Robinson. To my surprise, my dad and
some of those weird friends of his were the stars of the
show. I discovered that these "bohemians" had established
the first gallery for contemporary art in the city of New Orleans. The Orleans Gallery on Royal Street set the stage, or
better yet, stretched the canvas for the Arts District, CAC,
and even the recent revival of St. Claude Avenue. As I used
to say when I thought I knew more than I actually did,
"Who woulda thunk?"

Like most artists, my dad had a day job, a very successful

one. Over the years he developed more than sixty subdivisions. While we were off at school, my dad built roads, dug canals and ditches, cleared and planted trees, negotiated loans, and sold residential lots. After work, he would watch my little league practice. He'd then play Mr. Mom and serve us dinner, usually take-out Chinese or Popeye's fried chicken. (Cooking was not his strong suit.) We'd then watch football or classic movies. My dad is a big fan of *Casablanca*, *On the Waterfront*, and *A Man for All Seasons*. While we did our homework, or after we went to bed, he'd go to his other job and paint. He kept a cot in his studio just in case.

If my dad hadn't become an artist and developer, he could have easily exceled at a number of other professions. With his amazing eye and incredible aesthetics, he could have been an interior decorator (see his house), a landscape architect (see his property), or a fashion designer (see his wardrobe). He would have also made a pretty decent farmer. To this day, he keeps chickens and guinea-fowl and grows beautiful eggplants and figs.

Production is incredibly important to my father. He paints every day without fail. He still takes chances and makes mistakes. "It's the only way you learn," he likes to say. "You can't just talk about art; you have to make it!"

My dad, George Dunbar
in his studio

With my dad in 2014

The other day I came across a beautiful drawing tucked away in my dad's studio. It was from the 1970s. When I asked him why he had never shown it in a gallery, he said, "It looks too much like a Twombly. It's derivative. You need to get your own unique thumbprint on your work. People should be able to recognize it as yours from across the room." As for my dad's work, it is unmistakably his own. It is "a Dunbar."

They say creativity is for the young. Try telling that to

my Old Man. At ninety, he's more creative than ever. He just had a show with more than twenty-five original works. After the opening, he jumped on a plane to New York City. "That's where the action is," he said. "I want to see the Stella show at the new Whitney, check out Picasso's sculptures, and see what's going on in Chelsea. I need to find a little inspiration for my next show."

"I'm an old dude," my dad recently confessed. "I've been around a long time. I've learned a few things. And now, more than ever, I've got urgency. Let's go make some art!"

Whenever you ask my dad how he's doing, he always answers the same way: "I'm doing the best I can." For as long as I've known my dad—my entire life—"the best he can," in both art and life, is nothing short of extraordinary.

If it were not for my father, I would have never recovered from many of my falls. Yes, my dad is definitely my favorite artist. More importantly, he's my favorite person. He's my hero.

Of course, I am a bit biased.

The "Fall" that Ended Well

Disclaimer: My wife's version of this story may be wildly different.

The Stalker

My wife was a stalker.

Fortunately for me, I was the object of her affection. And, she was persistent.

We first met when I was fifteen and she was twelve. (Little did she know, but I had already reached my height potential.) The director of my dad's gallery was dating her father. Our families would occasionally get together for art shows and social events.

One time, Lucia came to our house for a party. Greeting my mother at the door, she said, "Hello Mrs. Dunbar, my name is Lucia."

My mom looked at her quizzically and proclaimed, "Welcome Isabella!"

"I'm sorry Mrs. Dunbar, but my name is Lucia," said Lucia.

Like Meryl Streep playing Anna Wintour, my mother corrected her, "Don't be silly darling, your name is Isabella."

(My mother thought that Lucia looked like the mod-

My future wife Lucia around
the time we met

el and actress, Isabella
Rossellini. For the rest
of her life, she referred
to Lucia as "Isabella.")

From grade school
through high school, Lu-
cia kept a diary. In it, she
had a list of her favorite
crushes. They includ-
ed older boys from the
neighborhood, actors
like Paul Newman and
Robert Redford, and almost all of Duran Duran.** I was
in the top ten, somewhere between John Taylor and Si-
mon Le Bon.

Lucia wasn't crazy about her last name, so she often
tried out ones from the list. I think she liked "Lucia Redford" the best.

A few years ago, I discovered her diary in a cardboard
box in the attic. There was an entire page dedicated to
"Mrs. Dunbar." Like Shelley Duvall running across Jack
Nicholson's working manuscript in *The Shining*, I found it
a tad disconcerting!

On a family trip to Florida one year, Lucia actually
tried to kiss me. Even though she was cute and I was a

---

* Lucia's Duran Duran poster is still in our attic. As for me, I had
crushes on Nastassja Kinski of snake poster fame, Elle McPherson of
Sports Illustrated cover fame, and Lola Granola from *Bloom County*.

dork, I ducked her advances. Like all boys of a certain age, I was only interested in older women. I was *The Graduate*, but unfortunately, all the Mrs. Robinsons** in Destin had absolutely no interest whatsoever.

When I moved to Durham, North Carolina, for college, Lucia's mother married a professor who taught at Chapel Hill. She sent Lucia to school at Durham Academy, which was just up the road from my dorm. On occasion, I would bump into her on campus. I told friends she was my stalker from New Orleans. She told friends I was the boy she would eventually marry.

Lucia had a serious boyfriend in high school. Her younger sister, Lauren was not a big fan. One day when the two of them were together, Lauren said, "You know, my sister will never marry you."

"Why is that?" asked the boyfriend.

"Because my sister prefers boys with brown eyes—boys like Folwell Dunbar."

After college, I joined the Peace Corps and moved to Ecuador. Lucia went to college in Colorado. I was pretty sure I would never see my stalker again.

After college, Lucia applied to graduate school and got into Smith and Tulane. Smith was her first choice, but Tulane was more affordable. She couldn't decide.

Lauren, who was visiting friends in New Orleans, ran into me at a party. She discovered that I was living in the city, teaching at Lucia's alma mater, single, and disappointingly short. She immediately called her sister and told her about my location, relationship status, and job.

** Just before I met Lucia, I dated a much older woman. Coincidentally, her name was, "Mrs. Robinson."

(Fortunately for me, she didn't mention my stature.) "You *have* to go to Tulane," she said. "It was meant to be!"

Lucia packed her bags and moved back to New Orleans. Yes, she was definitely a stalker!

Art for Arts' Sake

I was courting a young woman named Leslie. She worked at The French Connection on Decatur Street. Being a teacher and student at the time, I couldn't exactly afford new clothes; but I needed an excuse to visit the store. So, I went in once a week and bought a single item, socks, a tie, a belt.... After about three months, I owned my first suit. Now broke and out of excuses, I had no choice but to ask Leslie out. She agreed to meet me at the Contemporary Arts Center or CAC for Art for Arts' Sake. I was pumped up like a show dog—wearing an imported charcoal jacket with shoulder pads!

The CAC was packed. I scanned the room for Leslie, and eventually spotted her on the second floor. As I was walking up the stairs though, a woman I didn't know jumped in my path and yelled, "Are you Folwell Dunbar?!"

"Yes," I said, craning my neck to keep an eye on Leslie.

"THE Folwell Dunbar?!" she added.

"As far as I know," I said.

"I have a friend who is DYING to speak to you," she declared. "Her name is Lucia, and she knows your entire life story!"

Lucia was celebrating the end of her first semester exams with a friend. She had obviously had a few too many adult beverages. She stumbled up to me and, indeed, began to recount my entire life story.

Lucia was cute to be sure. She looked like, well, Isabella Rossellini, with dark bangs and stunning blue eyes. But, she was also babbling like an off-duty stenographer; and I had bought a &%$#ing suit!

As Lucia blathered on, I tried my best to break away. But I couldn't. Her monologue was like Fidel Castro's speech to the UN in 1960, epic and inescapable.

When she finally concluded, the CAC was practically empty. And Leslie was gone.

My father likes to remind me, "When all else fails, act like a gentleman." Considering the evening had definitely been a failure, I did the gentlemanly thing and offered to give Lucia a ride home. She said her car was parked just around the corner. But it wasn't. We spent the next hour and a half scouring the Warehouse District, but we couldn't find it. (I would later discover that Lucia was directionally challenged, and, was not a very good driver to boot: a bad combination for road trips by the way!)

Convinced the car had been stolen (it wasn't), I told Lucia we could ride the streetcar back to my place, and then I could drive her home.

To avoid talking to Lucia, I stuck my head out the window. As we rambled down St. Charles Avenue, I remember pulling it in periodically to avoid being decapitated by telephone poles and oak trees—which, by the way, may have been preferable to conversation.

I had a vintage 1964 Toyota Land Cruiser. The gas gauge (and several other things) didn't work, so I had to check the tank with a long bamboo pole. I was too embarrassed to do it in front of Lucia, so I just drove her home.

My future wife in front of my vintage Toyota Land Cruiser

Along the way, Lucia, now sober, mentioned the soundtrack to the 1987 film, *The Mission*. I loved the movie and the music. I was hoping to share a few songs with my class, but didn't have the album. Lucia did, but she told me she would have to dig it up. I asked her if we could make the exchange at a coffee shop the following day. She agreed.

Driving back to my place well after midnight, I, of course, ran out of gas.

Apart from getting a CD of Ennio Morricone's incredible score, the meeting at the coffee shop was a complete disaster. This time, I was the one who babbled. I went on and on about the historical significance of the yoke, not the homophone in the middle of an egg, but rather the contraption you place around the neck of a beast of burden. I also brought up obscure books, Bob

Dylan lyrics, and random Louisiana trivia. On the topic of soundtracks, I mentioned *Reservoir Dogs*. "I hear the director, Quentin Tarentino, has a new film out," I said. To my surprise, Lucia suggested that we see it together.

Our second "date" wasn't much better. I had won a couple of movie passes in a trivia contest at a local video store, so I took Lucia to see *Pulp Fiction* at Canal Place. When we got to the theatre, I sat down two seats away. Lucia looked at me like a Rorschach Test. I explained, "It's not you, I just don't like to be distracted."

On the ride home, I had to stop to check the gas. I'm pretty sure Lucia was not impressed.

When I dropped her off, I wasn't sure what to say. I figured I had finally scared off my stalker. At last, I blurted out, "My dad's having an opening next Saturday at Gallery Simone Stern. You should go."

A Process of Elimination

I ended up inviting five different women to my dad's show. There was Robin, a hippie throwback with rings on her toes and flowers in her hair; Leslie from The French Connection (I wore the suit); Bethany, a redhead who was at least five inches taller than me; Maimie, my childhood sweetheart; and Lucia, my childhood stalker.

I was in a romantic funk at the time. My confidence and expectations were at an all-time low. I assumed only one or two would actually show, and that neither one would consider it a date. I was wrong on both counts. They ALL showed, and they ALL thought they were with me!

It was like a bad episode of *Three's Company*, only there

were six of us.

At first, I tried to manage the mayhem—juggle the balls as it were. I had friends run interference, I made up all kinds of implausible excuses, blew smoke, and hung mirrors.

At one point, my dad came up to me and asked, "So son, who *exactly* are you here with?"

"I'm really not sure," I confessed. "Do you have a preference?"

Like Plato in prison, I guzzled wine like hemlock.

As the night pro(re)gressed, three of my five "dates" caught on to the ruse. They looked at me with contempt and exited the gallery. When the opening closed, only Lucia and Robin remained.

Robin suggested that we go dancing. She even offered to drive. I invited a few friends, including Lucia.

At Café Istanbul on Frenchmen Street, I could hardly stand. The red wine had turned my legs into wet noodles. I danced, or more accurately, clung to Lucia, and then to Robin, and then to Lucia. While propping myself up with Lucia, I noticed Robin across the room. She obviously wasn't happy; she had figured things out. She glared at me, smashed a beer bottle on the hardwood floor, fired off a few choice expletives, and stormed out of the bar.

By process of elimination, Lucia was now officially "my date."

We bummed a ride from a friend, sat in the back seat —and kissed.***

*** Several years later, we were telling the story of how we met to a group of friends. When I mentioned the five dates, Lucia looked shocked and horrified. "Are you serious?!" she said. "What kind of guy would actually do such a thing?!" Realizing my gaffe, I said, "Well of course, the other four weren't *really* dates.…"

Kissing my future wife

The CAC Revisited

I was teaching middle and high school history at an all-girls school. Not surprisingly, my students were far more interested in my relationship status than studying history. Like gifted grifters, they would use all kinds of ploys to divert the discussion toward my love life. They would say things like, "So, Mr. Dunbar, could you tell us again why we should never discuss the importance of the yoke on a first date?" "Bob Dylan sure has a lot of protest songs! Does he have any that capture your love for Lucia?" And, "The Japanese caught us off guard at Pearl Harbor. How do you plan to surprise Lucia when you pop the question?"

Being a hopeless romantic and a sucker for tangents, I often indulged them. Keep in mind, this was long before high-stakes testing. And, I enjoyed the challenge of bringing a tangent full-circle.

Over time, OUR relationship became THEIR project. So, when I told them I was planning to propose, it was like the Grand Finale. They were giddy like, well, schoolgirls. They told me it HAD to happen at the CAC, it HAD to be a huge surprise, the ring HAD to be beautiful, and there HAD to be flowers, lots and lots of flowers. I agreed—and gave the class an "A."

Through my dad, I knew the curator of the CAC. I asked him to set up a pedestal on the second floor where we had (re)met two years earlier. My mom had given me her diamond ring. I placed it on the pedestal and scattered dozens of red roses on the floor. Beneath the ring, I placed a brass nameplate inscribed with "Mrs. Dunbar?"

I told Lucia a mutual friend of ours was having a show at the CAC. I even had him create a fake invitation and send it to us.

Walking around the gallery, Lucia became frustrated. "I don't see Michael's work anywhere," she complained. "And, there's nobody here. Maybe we got the wrong date?"

"Be patient," I said. "I think his work is in the next room."

Rounding the corner, Lucia saw the pedestal and roses. Finding it a bit disturbing, she dismissed it as just a "bad installation," turned away and kept walking.

"Maybe the flower thing back there was his?" I suggested. "We should take a closer look."

"No," she said, "that thing was scary. It couldn't possibly be Michael's work."

"Let's go back," I insisted, "just in case…"

When she saw the ring on the pedestal, she stopped in

My wife and her sister at our wedding

her tracks—and, to my horror, said absolutely nothing.

I hadn't planned to say anything myself. My cocon-spirators at school had assured me that the plaque would suffice. Instead, she waited for me to ask, and I waited for her to answer. Like the moments before a gunfight in a Spaghetti Western, the silence was palpable.

Finally, I shakily drew and muttered, "Would you marry me?"

"I was hoping for an emerald cut," she said with a smile, "but, I do like the name. The answer is 'Yes.'" ****

**** On the ride home, Lucia asked, "So, what did my dad say?"
"Your dad?" I said.
"Yes," she said. "You *did* ask my dad…"

Epilogue

Like most couples, Lucia and I have experienced any number of "falls" over the years. There were crocodiles in Jamaica and bad brakes in Colima, Hurricane Katrina and numerous career calamities, a bad medical diagnosis and, of course, FAMILY! Through it all though, we've managed to stay together. Falling in love is not a bad "fall" at all!

About the Author

Fol·well \ fól-wel \ n, pl. Folwells [from the Cajun Faux and Weeeeeee] This highly endangered and elusive species (folwellius dunbarian, estimated population: 1. Common names include Foz, Fu, Fuzzy, Foly and Fu-Bear) was first discovered in the mid 1960s along the creosote shores of Bayou Bonfouca. Genetic research has shown that it was first conceived in Mexico, carried north by a band of Olmec nomads, and finally deposited beneath a bald cypress tree in the Honey Island Swamp. Legend has it that an osprey had landed there with a cottonmouth in its talons. The young child was then placed in a pirogue and set adrift. He was soon discovered by a den of aquatic reptilian royalty and nursed to maturity by a particularly handsome, nine-foot she-gator. Once weaned, the young Folwell began feeding on nutria rats, water hyacinth, and other vile, introduced "exotic" species. Eventually, the young hominid left its adopted home and sojourned northward to the glaciated reaches of Massachusetts for some good, wholesome Puritanical book learnin'. After four frostbitten years of preppy, intellectual enlightenment, Folwell carpetbagged it back south to the gothic tobacco barns of Durham, North Carolina. After another "cough, cough," four years of higher order thinking and lower order grappling at Duke University, he ventured to the hinterlands of South America. In Zhumar, Ecuador (pop. 54 on a good day!), he culled rogue sheep, raised rainbow trout in earthen ponds, cooked guinea pigs over an open fire, kept "killer" bees, and drank lots of spittle-tainted *chi-*

cha and kerosene-toxic *trago*. Once again though, after almost three years of Andean bliss and Atawalpa's revenge, the wander-lustful neotropical migrant set off. He trekked along the *Ruta Maya*, past the land of United Fruit and through the fields of the Zapatistas, until he finally settled in the true "Banana Republic" of Louisiana. In the Big Queasy, he taught Ancient, U.S., and World History, Spanish, and first grade. He studied at Tulane and juggled on Decatur Street, until, once again, he took flight. Landing in the virtual reality of the Research Triangle Park, he helped found a school for techno-savvy cyber children, coached wrestling, and visited countless, generic shopping malls. After only two years in CARY (Concentrated Area of Relocated Yankees), he was drawn back to the Big Queasy by the ethereal beat of Satchmo, Sidney Bechet, and of course Professor Longhair. There, he set out on a quest for comprehensive whole-school reform, a.k.a. Peace Corps with a paycheck. He scooped and delivered dollops of PD, scribbled reams of educational, jargon-infused drivel, founded an arts-integrated school, and beat the drum loudly for improved teaching and learning. His musings on education and life can be found in numerous publications, including *Edutopia*, *Independent School*, *Teacher Magazine*, *Middle Ground*, *Our Children*, *Pacific Standard*, *School Administrator*, and *The Lens*. Folwell, his very tolerant wife Lucia, and their dog, Mole (after the Mexican sauce and not the rodent) live in a decrepit shotgun doublewide, two blocks from Desire, downriver and on the wrong side of the tracks. They can be found fighting the *stupids*, social working, and generally barking around.

Folwell can be reached at fldunbar@icloud.com

With thanks

To family members, friends and colleagues for joining me on many of the misadventures, to my parents, Jane and George Dunbar for trying to keep me safe, to Rita Whitehead and Bill Poirot for stepping in when my parents weren't there, to Lisa Ellis, Ricky Favor, Susan Geier, Scott Saltzman, Adam Newman, and others for editorial and design support, to David Sullivan for creating the flip book animation, to the folks at Via NolaVie for previewing many of the stories, and to my wife, Lucia for being incredibly patient.